BEHIND COLLECTIONS®

Graphic Design and Promotion for Fashion Brands.

First published and distributed by
viction workshop ltd

viction:ary

viction workshop ltd
Unit C, 7/F, Seabright Plaza, 9-23 Shell Street,
North Point, Hong Kong
Url: www.victionary.com
Email: we@victionary.com
 www.facebook.com/victionworkshop
 www.twitter.com/victionary_
 www.weibo.com/victionary

Edited and produced by viction:ary

Concept & art direction by Victor Cheung
Book design by viction workshop ltd
Cover image: Page Three Hundred MMXIV Fall/Winter
Collection, photographed by Alberto Raviglione

ISBN 978-988-12227-4-9
Printed and bound in China

The cooperation between graphic and fashion design is a very inspiring one. As a graphic designer it is always fascinating to be a part of the launch of a new fashion collection and to help bring the designer's vision to life. The invitation to a new runway show can be seen as the fuse of the firework that will be the actual presentation. It is a challenge to make sure that the theme of the show is visible in the invitation in a very subtle way, so that it works as a teaser, giving the audience a small glimpse of what is to come. The invitation already has to slightly unfold the theme of the collection, which will be revealed in the actual runway show.

As a graphic designer, I always had the privilege of working together with fashion designers that have a very strong affection with visual arts and love to be inspired by it, just like I find inspiration in the world of arts. In my graphic work there are a lot of strong references to the arts, and it is always a pleasure to work together with people who share that passion. A joint love of the work of Joseph Beuys for example was the start of a very successful cooperation with fashion brand A.F.Vandevorst.

Another parallel between the worlds of fashion and graphic design is the choice of materials, which is of the highest importance in both the collections and the artwork. All the designers I work with choose to present their products in the most exclusive way, leaving me with the challenge to create something unique and yet relevant to represent their collection. I draw a lot of inspiration from visual arts, but also old type specimens, visual poetry and worn out letters you find in the streets. I discovered this way of looking through the magazine Typographica. Articles from people like Robert Brownjohn and Dieter Roth really opened my eyes and introduced me to the world of typography.

I personally insist on following the whole process from the idea to the final execution, so that the actual design is the result of an intense interaction between myself and the fashion designer. For me it is of the utmost importance to follow up the printing process very closely. I often combine conventional and artisan printing techniques, and my choice of material is not always the most evident. Once I printed on goldfoil for Dries Van Noten, and recently I produced an invitation for A.F.Vandevorst, which was printed on an actual bird's feather. Every single printer I asked assured me that it would be impossible to execute, but we pushed through and managed to succeed after all.

This example shows to me the great challenge that lies in graphic design for fashion brands. Clients working in a creative industry often have very high demands, but at the same time are very open to all kinds of ideas, creating the perfect circumstances for graphic designers to be daring and bold in their designs. For me that means looking for original materials and printing techniques, that might not be possible to use with clients outside the fashion industry.

To visualise inspiration in this way is both a challenge and a privilege.

FOREWORD BY

JELLE JESPERS GRAPHIC DESIGNER

TRANSLATION BY

ANS VROOM

To us freedom-loving graphic designers, there seems to be no better more auspicious and exciting work than taking on a job for a client from the fashion business. Fashion in general conveys the impression of being an enormously huge adventure playground for all sorts of creatives – from the fashion designers themselves, to tailors, dressmakers, photographers, stylists, art directors, illustrators, hair and make-up artists and last but not least graphic designers. And of course there lies a big chunk of truth in this assumption. Did we not all choose to work in the creative field of design in order to live out our imaginative outbursts?

After all, it is fashion that brings creatives from different fields to collaborate. Whether it is haute couture runway-shows, experimental store interiors, extravagant fashion shoots or ground-breaking concepts for fashion magazines – it's always the result of successful cooperations rather than the work of an individual. The same principle usually applies when developing the visual identity and branding for fashion designers – after all, the clients themselves are creative libertines and hence it is also their thoughts that have great influence on the final result.

It is fashion, that does not only allow, but often even demands to exploit artistic freedom in order to push the boundaries while many times crossing and redefining them. Trends are set by sailing close to the wind instead of docking in the port. The fast-paced rhythm of fashion not only calls for frequent changes of visual languages but also requires extraordinary conceptions. Each seasonal collection needs to be communicated and presented to an eager and expectant audience – each collection's visual appearance needs to strike, stand out, and attract the consumers' attentions. Fashion audience is spoilt for choice and attention spans are short. Again it is the fashion industry, that evokes ground-breaking imagery by hiring top-notch studios, taking the risk and giving carte blanche to contentious and provocative artists. Many times it is the upsetting, highly controversial campaigns that cause an outcry but thus go down in history.

Talking about big players out there we shouldn't forget to mention that everyone in the business begins in a small way. The fashion business is for sure one of the toughest fields for start-ups – we've seen many young creatives come and go – but at the same time it offers great perspectives. You won't earn much as an upcoming fashion designer, fashion photographer, stylist or graphic artist, but fashion definitely always offers a great public platform to prove your skills. It's often the young design generation that comes out with staggering creations, it's photographers shooting with minimal pay that bring surprises because of their fresh views from different perspectives, it's small design studios that reinvent visual languages in unexpected ways, and it's experimental low-budget workarounds that in the end bring forth astonishing results.

Reading through my first four paragraphs I am pretty amazed myself how excessively positive this ode to fashion turned out to be. The fashion business is for sure divisive, sometimes cruel, sometimes affectionate. But it is a fact that fashion does play an inherent role in all of our daily lives. It is also a fact that fashion-related creative outputs are special, forward-thinking, groundbreaking and innovative. So let's sit back for a moment and enjoy the international work samples featured in this book. May the inspirational force be with you.

FOREWORD
BY

BEN WITTNER
GRAPHIC DESIGNER, COFOUNDER OF EPS51

AD: Art direction

CD: Creative direction

CG: Computer graphics

CL: Client

CO: Project coordination

CP: Copywriting

CR: Special credits

DE: Design

ED: Editing

FM: Film

HA: Hair

IL: Illustration

MA: Make-up/cosmetics

MO: Modelling

PD: Production

PH: Photography

PT: Printing

RT: Retouching

SE: Setting & installation

SO: Sound

ST: Styling

INVITATION ITSELF HAS SIMPLY BECOME AN ART PIECE. AS ALWAYS FOR FASHION, IT'S THE ULTIMATE PLAYGROUND TO EXPLORE. TO BUILD ANTICIPATION AND EXPECTANCY, BRANDS HAVE STARTED TO MAKE THEIR OWN RULES. PLASTIC CASE, DRIED PRESSED FLOWER, A CLOTHING ITEM AND BOARD GAME WERE ALL USED CREATE STRIKING INVITATIONS. ATTENTION TO DETAILS IS THE KEY; BY CLEVERLY INTERPRETING DESIGNER'S CREATION AND DEVELOP IT INTO TANGIBLE OBJECTS AND VISUAL EFFECTS, OFTEN A LOT OF POTENTIAL GUESTS ARE WON OVER.

FROM PROMOTION TO INVITATIONS

DRIES VAN NOTEN

MEN'S COLLECTION SPRING / SUMMER 2014
THURSDAY 27TH JUNE 2013 AT 7PM

LA HALLE FREYSSINET, 55 BOULEVARD VINCENT AURIOL, 75013 PARIS.
METRO: 6 CHEVALERET

COMMUNICATION +33 1 42 74 44 07

DRIES VA

WOMEN'S COLLECTION S
WEDNESDAY 25TH OF SE

LA HALLE FREYSSINET, 55 BOULEVA
METRO: 6 CH

COMMUNICATION

DRIES VAN NOTEN MEN'S & WOMEN'S SS14 SHOW INVITATION

The gleaming invitation in Byzantine gold responds to Dries Van Noten SS14's theme for both men's and women's collections. The invitations to respective shows can be seen as one, with two thin gold foil rectangles printed at slightly tiled angles on the men's card. And reversed on the women's card, with show details screenprinted in black.

DE: Jelle Jespers

CL: Dries Van Noten

PH: Ann Vallé

DRIES VAN NOTEN

WOMEN'S COLLECTION SPRING/SUMMER 2014
WEDNESDAY 25ᵀᴴ OF SEPTEMBER 2013 AT 3PM

FREYSSINET, 55 BOULEVARD VINCENT AUR...
METRO: 6 CHEVALERET
...MUNICATION +33 1 4...

MER 2014
AT 3PM

JRIOL, 75013 PARIS.

7

DRIES VAN NOTEN SS14 ANNOUNCEMENT CARD

The golden gleam in Dries Van Noten's SS14 collection lingers on its announcement card. Echoing the show's invitations in gold foil (P.010), this subtle shimmer on laminated paper reminds guests of the storey-high backdrop flowing alongside men's runway, while the leporello bound is drawn from folding screens bedecking women's show.

DE: Jelle Jespers

CL: Dries Van Noten

PH: Lea Colombo, Bache Jespers, Tommy Ton (Fashion shot), Ann Vallé (Product shot)

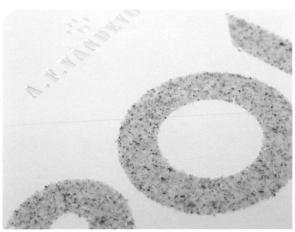

A.F.VANDEVORST SS14 SHOW INVITATION, NEW YEAR CARD & LOOKBOOK

Started by Belgian husband and wife duo, A.F.Vandevorst welcomes their 15th anniversary by recreating some of the couple's most cherished pieces in SS14. Set apart for their storytelling prowess, An Vandevorst and Filip Arickx conjure up a fun day by the beach with sea sand plastered on models, showcasing pieces as well as typography of the invitation. The design also extends onto the label's New Year card and lookbook.

DE: Jelle Jespers

CL: A.F.Vandevorst

PH: Ann Vallé

ZAMBESI AW13 VIP INVITATION

New Zealand fashion house Zambesi has been delivering designs of
individuality and dark edgy aesthetic since 1979. AW13 is a season in which
they explore vintage sensibility and layering. Their invitation is also an
exploration of layers — a square-cut in multiple angular folds that evolves as
it opens and set off the yellow and black checkerboard prints of the featured
key pieces.

DE: Sean Walker

CL: Zambesi

CR: Marissa Findlay (PH), Jordan
Barrie, Anmarie Botha @Red11 (MO)

ZAMBESI
since 1979

please join us for an
inspiring evening in
celebration of our
winter 2013 collections

wednesday 27th march, 6pm.
107 customhouse quay,
wellington.

rsvp:
wellington@zambesi.co.nz

MASSEY
UNIVERSITY
UNIVERSITY OF NEW ZEALAND
fab lab
wgtn

INVIVO

NEW ZEALAND WINE

HONOR FW14 SHOW INVITATION

Honor is a women's luxury brand that infuses the world of modern fashion with the nostalgia of an old-world atelier. The label's 2014 Fall/Winter runway show presents a versatile romantic beauty from the sixties. Its invitation tries to envision such organic elegance with choice of materials — the front a mirrored gold foil debossed with the Honor logo, contrasting beautifully with the rich walnut wood on the back.

DE: High Tide

CL: Honor

Come and see ou[r]
store at Salone de[...]
We'd love to see [...]

Via Ventura, 15
Lambrate
Milan

cosstores.com

COS

Thank you for visiting our
pop-up concept store!

COS

We're celebrating
10/04/13
19.00–23.00

COS 2013 SALONE DEL MOBILE INSTALLATION INVITATION & FLYER

A collaboration between COS and creative studios INT Works and Bonsoir
Paris resulted in an installation that was a comma to frantic city life for
visitors to Milan's renowned Salone Del Mobile. Their approach, mirrors the
international label's design ethos through modular components constructed
in a functional and visually lightweight way. To forge consistent aesthetics
INT works designed the invitation and flyer using cork boards dipped in white
while Bonsoir Paris used a balance of tactile materials within the installation.

DE: INT Works

CL: COS

CR: Bonsoir Paris (SE),
Owen Richards (PH)

MAGIC JOHNSTON 2012 DESIGNER SALE INVITATION & PROMOTION

Magic Johnston's designer sale features versatile indie fashion labels from local and around the world. Adopting the Australian design and cultural space's signature hue, visual identity for the Designer Sale is a simple sticker book depiction that delivers key info in a straightforward layout and playful typeface, which is applied onto signage and collateral.

DE: Studio SP-GD

CL: Magic Johnston

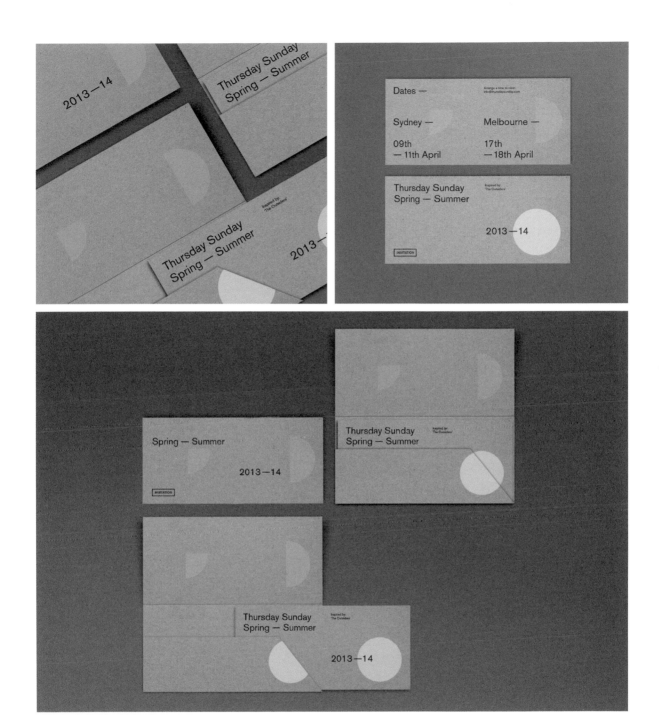

THURSDAY SUNDAY SS13-14 SHOW INVITATION

Started by Iris Cuaresma and Mara Tonetti — good friends since grade four,
Thursday Sunday is a Melbourne-based label that emphasises natural fibres
and minimal lines. Invites for its Spring/Summer 13-14 collection is created in
response to exclusiveness. Using grey cardboard that resonates with chosen
palette, incomplete pie shapes are tokens of discrete of the unrevealed
collection to create excitement.

DE: Studio SP-GD

CL: Thursday Sunday

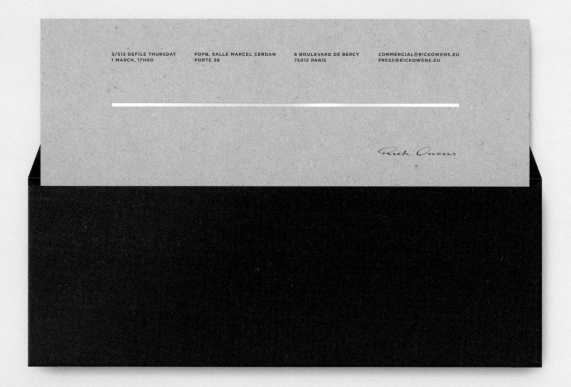

RICK OWENS 2012-14 SHOW INVITATION

Various invitations were designed for the Rick Owens' shows at the Paris Fashion Weeks between 2012 and 2014. Sized 297 x 105 mm, the cut is chosen by the fashion radical himself, who used it for all of his previous invitations. Silk printing, embossing and gilding are applied onto the 3mm stock to enhance texture. With the fixed canvas, creativity is still unlimited with the orientation, alignment, typography and printing techniques left to play with.

DE: Notter + Vigne

CL: Rick Owens

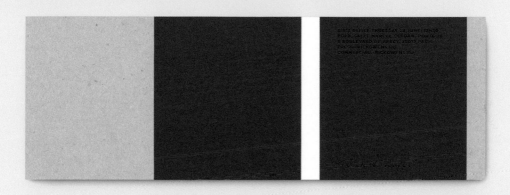

ANN DEMEULEMEESTER SS09 SHOW INVITATION

Enclosed in a standard white envelope is a 96-page miniature publication telling details of Ann Demeulemeester's SS09 Paris show. Eschewing colours, the little book stays in line with the signature palette of this deconstructionist label originated from Antwerp. The page content goes blank after page 29, what comes after is up to reader's imagination.

DE: Jelle Jespers, Patrick Robyn

CL: Ann Demeulemeester

PH: Ann Vallé

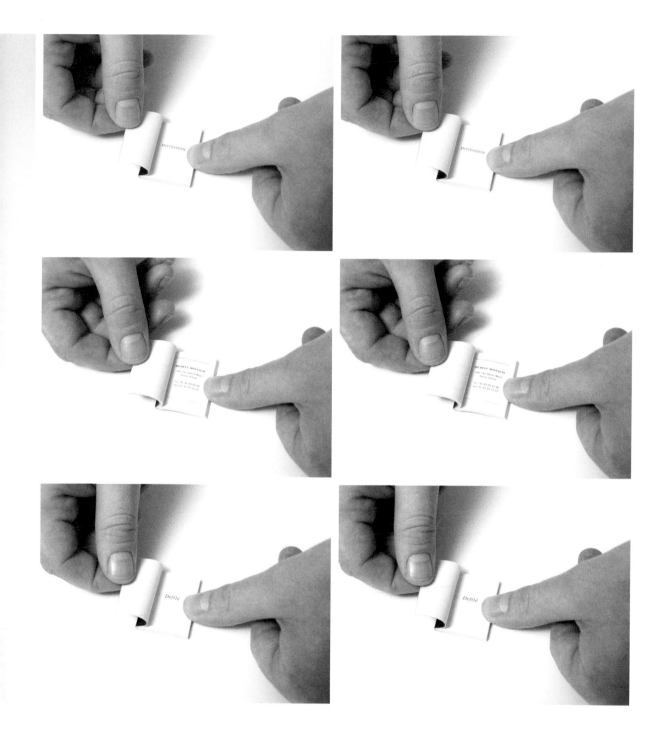

DRIES VAN NOTEN MEN'S SS15 SHOW INVITATION

The gracile figures of male dancers as well as their on and off stage wardrobe is what brought about Dries Van Noten men's SS15 collection. Invitation for its runway show is designed to convey the dancers' airiness in movement. Unfurling a 28 gram paper folded twice reveals a translucent tracing paper that delivers show info, and a grand cutout of the letter "R" in flaming red — a tribute to the ballet legend Rudolf Nureyev.

DE: Jelle Jespers

CL: Dries Van Noten

PH: Ann Vallé

DRIES VAN NOTEN WOMEN'S AW14-15 SHOW INVITATION

Taking on a 19th century book design, these paperboard invitations point guests of Dries Van Noten Women's show to the direction of Hôtel de Ville, a Parisian administrative building that houses decor of the same era. Classical elegance crafted through layout and typography is electrified by dashing lily orange and magenta at the thick rims. The colours addresses swirling optic art prints and 3D flower sculptures that pop their way through the collection.

DE: Jelle Jespers

CL: Dries Van Noten

PH: Ann Vallé

MENBUR FW14-15 FAIRS SEASON INVITATION

A poster style invitation for the Menbur Fall/Winter 14-15 invitation can be folded into a letter and slip comfortably into an envelope. The subject was plain to the recipients' eyes as captions were printed directly across the envelope's back. The subtlety of black printing over pearlised paper sets off the crafted silhouette and sparkly details of Menbur's shoe.

DE: Play&Type

CL: Menbur

PH: Raúl Ruz

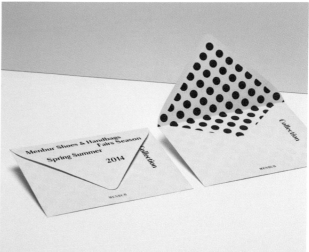

MENBUR SS14 FAIRS SEASON INVITATION

Appropriate for spring and summer, vibrant red was used all over the invitation to Menbur's private exhibition worldwide. Centred around the red polka dot shoe from its SS14 collection, the edge of the invitation and the caption are all filled with same shade of red. Also, a little touch in details can be spotted inside the envelope as red polka dots are printed inside, which matches the shoe.

DE: Play&Type

CL: Menbur

PH: Raúl Ruz

DRIES VAN NOTEN
Women's collection summer 2015
Wednesday, 24th September 2014 at 3pm
Grand Palais Porte A
3, avenue du Général Eisenhower
75008 Paris

Métro : 1/13 Champs - Elysées Clemenceau
communications +33 1 42 74 44 07

DRIES VAN NOTEN WOMEN'S SS15 SHOW INVITATION

Dries Van Noten sent out breaths of genuine freshness for their women's SS15
show. Visible through a transparent plastic case, lush Icelandic moss underlined
the pastoral carpet, a highlight on the runway that paid tribute to John Everett
Millais who's Van Noten's muse. The woodland setting recreated a scene in
Millais' *Ophelia* where the Hamlet character was depicted tranquilly drifting
before she drowned in a Danish river. The rug was handmade by Argentinian
artist Alexandra Kehayogloua, as Van Noten specially commissioned for the show.

DE: Jelle Jespers

CL: Dries Van Noten

PH: Ann Vallé

LIBERTY LONDON SS12 PRESS DAY INVITATION

Liberty is an iconic luxury department store in London. Invites for its 2012 Spring/Summer's launch takes inspiration from the season's runway trends — eclectic colours and floral prints. Dainty dried flowers are placed on acetate sheets of bright colours to create an arresting tone-on-tone palette, which is set off by serif typeface in contrasting hues.

DE: Laura Lé Vandenbergh

CL: Liberty London

AZEDE JEAN-PIERRE SS14 SHOW INVITATION

Azede Jean-Pierre's 2014 Spring/Summer collection is lavished with inspiration from nature. Playfully interpreting the roles of members often out of spotlight (insects and deep sea animals), the design evolves from wild aesthetic with functionality in mind as nature does. Invitation for its runway show is a box set embedded with beetle specimens in clear plastic resin blocks. The gift from nature simultaneously serves as a reminder of the show.

DE: Joseph Veazey

CL: Azede Jean-Pierre

AZEDE JEAN-PIERRE FW14 SHOW INVITATION

For a womenswear label that celebrates sensual femininity, Azede Jean-Pierre's FW14 runway show invitation looks austere, but not lack of warmth. Enclosed in a grey mailer package, it comes as a black knit hat with the date and time embroidered on top, whereas the RSVP is disguised as a price tag. Models wore similar knit hats on runway. Also, rich texture and earthy dark palette of the season are inspired by aerial views of unique landscapes.

DE: Joseph Veazey

CL: Azede Jean-Pierre

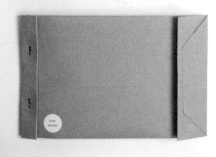

AZEDE JEAN-PIERRE SS11 DIRECT MAIL

Marking Azede Jean-Pierre's debut as a fashion designer, AJP's Spring/
Summer 2011 collection was brought to public attention with over 50 promotional
sets entirely made by hand. Black, berry, soft blush, and cream — the palette
that accented the pack articulated the colours that was going to unleash AJP
women's feminine divine. Contained in the box included a bundle of loose look
cards, a disk, and a price point guide.

DE: Joseph Veazey

CL: Azede Jean-Pierre

PH: Jamie Hopper

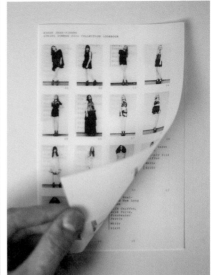
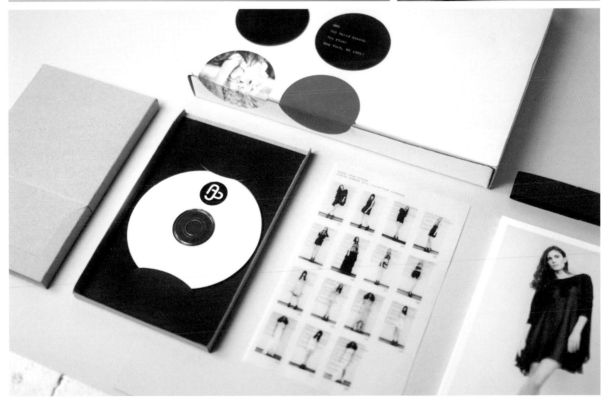

VOGUE LIMITED EDITION GIFT BOX

Skillfully designed and made by hand in an edition of 100, the leather pouch was sent out to Dutch celebrities such as Viktor & Rolf and Doutzen Kroes to coincide with the launch of Vogue Netherlands. The significance of the occasion and craftsmanship are matched with a luxury paper box. While subtleties contrasted the tactility of the design, an elegant white and grey tone was used for a simple, iconic appeal.

AD & DE: ...,staat creative agency

CL: Vogue Netherlands

LACOSTE MAISONS FRANÇAISES PRESS RELEASE

Lacoste's 80th anniversary is blessed with tailor-made tokens of congratulation from ten fellow premium French brands. Inspired by Lacoste's legendary crocodile, the all-star ensemble of precious objects from the likes of Hermès, Fauchon and Boucheron is documented as press release in a simple white case. Each member of the Maisons Françaises collection is introduced on an individual card with unique story written at the back.

DE: Acmé Paris

CL: Lacoste

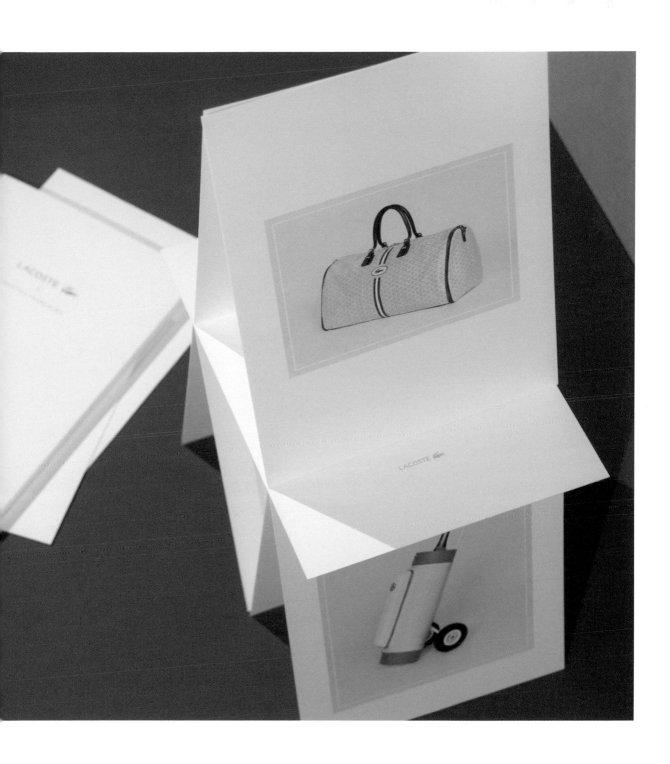

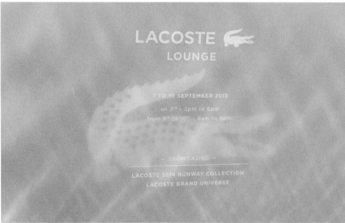

LACOSTE SS14 SHOWCASE INVITATION & PRESS KIT

Inspired by the idea of limits and being in and out of bounds like a tennis match, designer Felipe Oliveira Baptista devises a tone-on-tone palette with the exploration of transparency that adds to the sheer beauty of Lacoste's SS14 collection. Frame-stitched in a translucent matte package, its printed collateral stays in tune with the season's design by conveying lightness in mint and soothing minimalist aesthetic with an urban edge.

DE: Acmé Paris

CL: Lacoste

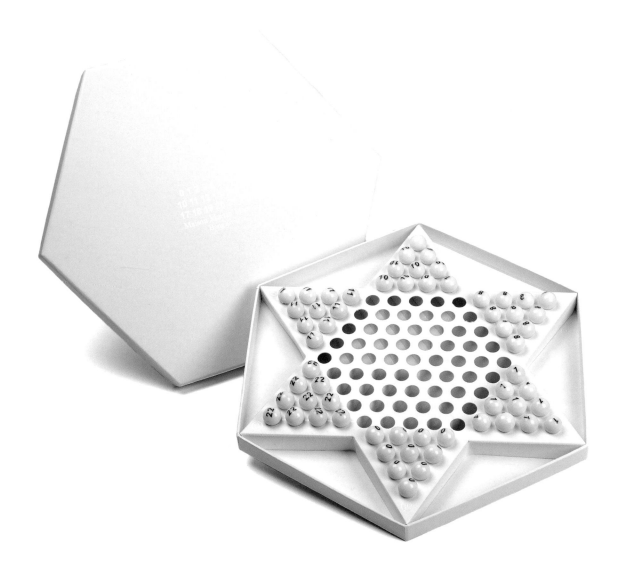

MAISON MARTIN MARGIELA CHINESE CHEQUERS SET

Maison Martin Margiela is noted for its progressive aesthetic and experimental approach towards fashion. Also touching on lifestyle goods, MMM collaborates with Hong Kong-based fashion group I.T in 2012 to reinterpret the Chinese Chequers into a limited Gift with Purchase. The blanched classic game set comes with numbered chess pieces that denotes how MMM name its product ranges.

DE: I.T APPARELS LTD.

CL: Maison Martin Margiela Paris

BYBROWN RAINDRESS LAUNCH INVITATION

Put forward by Amsterdam-based label Bybrown, Bybrown Raindress is a versatile garment to elegantly dress up for the rain. Enveloped in a poster, its launch invitation is screenprinted onto translucent paper stock to imply the rain. The poster is printed inside-out in minimalistic greyscale in line with the label's approach. Unfolding it not only uncloaks the details of the event but also the design of the Raindress.

DE: Occult Studio

CL: Bybrown

PH: Jasper Abels

ESCORPION SS13 SHOW INVITATION

Founded in 1929, Escorpion is a label specialised in women's knitwear weaved by the latest textile technology. Invitation for its Spring/Summer 2013 collection adopts a blanched and clean layout that resonates the bare hues applied onto each piece of the season. Overlaid on the styling shot, Escorpion's logotype is the prominent feature centring the invite, which is dashed with pale paint strokes to add to its texture.

DE: Play&Type

CL: Escorpion

PH: Raúl Ruz

SITA MURT FW13-14 PRESS RELEASE

Focusing on the essence of knitwear, Sita Murt's Fall/Winter 2013-14 runway show in Madrid presents a sensual and bold look for modern women. Stitch-sealed in kraft paper, its press release is simultaneously a sample catalogue. Unfolding the publication first unveils textual narrative, then a showcase of textures and colours for the season dominating each grid.

DE: Clase Bcn

CL: Sita Murt

ROBERT GELLER SS11 SHOW INVITATION & POSTER

ROBERT GELLER's Spring/Summer 2011 collection was inspired by the youth of the 1960s and 1970s. For the first time, various shades of red are introduced into the collection to speak to the passion and courage that marked the era's youth movement. With the label's rectangle logo presented as a square border, its invitation and poster are robust and bold in blazing red. The invitation is available in English and German, a tribute to Berlin's student movement.

DE: STUDIO NEWWORK

CL: ROBERT GELLER

ROBERT GELLER AW12 SHOW INVITATION

As previewed on the invitation poster, ROBERT GEI LER's 2012 Autumn/
Winter runway show leads guests to a country path where ingeniously suited
gentlemen walk the walk. The New York-based label presents a tailored
collection with playful twists — wide-brimmed hats, baggy trousers and two-
toned details, which is communicated through duo colour blocks of blue and
white that divides the poster.

DE: STUDIO NEWWORK

CL: ROBERT GELLER

ROBERT GELLER AW13 SHOW INVITATION & RUNWAY SET

ROBERT GELLER's Autumn/Winter 2013 collection muses over the vibe of Berlin in the 1920s. Bold enough to stand alone in each folded panel, solid black and white typography of the invite is printed in gritty texture with a sense of severity as seen in German expressionist films that were produced at the time. A distorted reality is created at the runway, drawing from film sets of the artistic genre while maintaining ROBERT GELLER's sense of poetic romance.

DE: STUDIO NEWWORK

CL: ROBERT GELLER

ROBERT GELLER SS13 SHOW INVITATION

French photographer Sarah Moon's moody, painterly images of beaches were a touchstone of Robert Geller's SS13 collection. Dreariness of her landscape blends in seamlessly with ROBERT GELLER's aesthetics and permeates the collection as well as its invitation. Set in an austere monotone, its playful typeface placement is backgrounded with a foggy and blurry image alluding to the photographer's signature soft focus.

DE: STUDIO NEWWORK

CL: ROBERT GELLER

ROBERT GELLER SS14 SHOW INVITATION & RUNWAY SET

ROBERT GELLER's Spring/Summer 2014 collection reflects on intellectual Russian youth in the 1980s, spotlights growing up in a crumbling Communist community that had produced the likes of Malevich and Vladimir Tatlin. Integrated basic geometric forms such as squares and lines in a limited palette of white, black and red is devised as a graphic representation of the era, which extends from invitation to the show set.

DE: STUDIO NEWWORK

CL: ROBERT GELLER

FIFTYTWO SHOWROOM SS14 MEN'S & WOMEN'S SS14 INVITATION

Fiftytwo is a New York-based fashion showroom representing a number of esteemed labels of womenswear, menswear, jewellery and accessories. Its Spring/Summer 2014 Men's market opening invitation is embellished with an abstract floral print reflective of the season's key trend. Invitation for Women's is a cheerful and poetic interpretation of a beach where splashes of Spring/Summer colours serves as a warm and fresh welcome to the showroom.

DE: STUDIO NEWWORK

CL: Fiftytwo Showroom

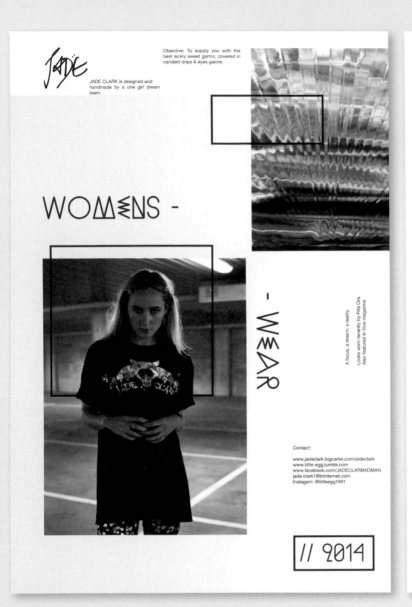

JADE CLARK POSTER SERIES

Jade Clark is a fashion design graduate from the UK's De Montfort University, whose design is worn by the likes of Rita Ora. With black text on a clean background to set off the dynamic colours and exhilarating aesthetic in her design, the series of posters is produced in 2013 to reflect key looks from her existing collections.

DE: Danielle Muntyan

CL: Jade Clark

JADE

Objective: To supply you with the best sickly sweet garmz, covered in candied drips & eyes galore.

WOMENS -

JADE CLARK is designed and handmade by a one girl dream team.

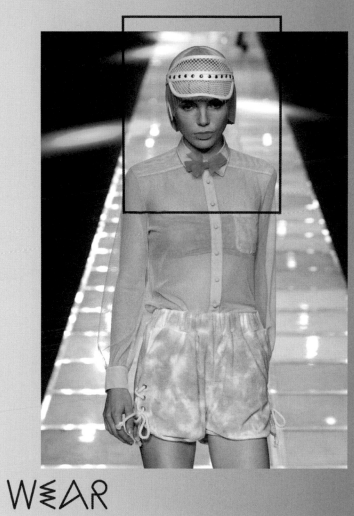

A focus, a dream, a reality.

Looks worn recently by Rita Ora. Also featured in Vice magazine.

- WEAR

Contact:

www.jadeclark.bigcartel.com/jadeclark
www.little-egg.tumblr.com
www.facebook.com/JADECLARBADMAN
jade.clark1@btinternet.com
Instagam: @littleegg1991

// 2014

IZZUE COLLECTION X WYMAN WONG SS12 LAUNCH CAMPAIGN

This special collaboration between celebrity figure Wyman Wong and cool urban brand, izzue, was meant to a fashion revolution. Done up with a paradoxical theme "I've Got Nothing to Wear", this line incorporated quirks and kitsch details that made its items simply bold and unique. To beat the drum for its launch, bills and catalogues printed on matching economical copy paper evoked a viral spread of hype around the city's streets.

DE: I.T APPARELS LTD.

CL: izzue

ORGANIC
John Patrick

ORGANIC
John Patrick

ORGANIC BY JOHN PATRICK RESORT 2014 PRINT ADVERTISING

Sustainable crafted basics are the focus of Organic by John Patrick's Resort collection. Capitalising on the brand's lookbook images with an aim to strengthen Organic's newly proposed brand image, Resort 2014's print advertisements once again had recourse to bright fresh crops for an utterly modern campaign. Set arrangements helped create a sense of ease as reflected in the collection's clothes.

DE: Tannia & Ahmad

CL: Organic by John Patrick

ORGANIC

John Patrick

organicbyjohnpatrick.com

THE FASHION WORLD OF JEAN PAUL GAULTIER INVITATION CONCEPT

The Fashion World of Jean Paul Gaultier is the first international exhibition and tribute to the French courtier's life work of unorthodox design. Anna Dormer Volgsten creates the invitation and poster for the world tour's last stop in Stockholm as an application assignment. A simple triangular extension on both sides of the card conjures a vivid image of the legendary corset Gaultier created for Madonna in 1990, which is also showcased in the exhibition.

DE: Anna Dormer Volgsten

CR: Beckmans College of Design

MELISSA X KARL LAGERFELD FW13 MEDIA KIT

Designing mini-collections for four consecutive seasons from 2013, Karl Lagerfled boosts fun and play in Melissa's exclusive shoe line. Media kit for their FW13 release gives the press a sweet taste of ice-creams in print, where the CD disguises as an eye-catching metallic scoop in matching magenta. It is to highlight one of the season's iconic designs, Melissa Incense, with a glittering ice-cream cone that fits right in place at the back of the heel.

DE: The Strangely Good

CL: Melissa Shoes Singapore by Enviably Me Pte Ltd

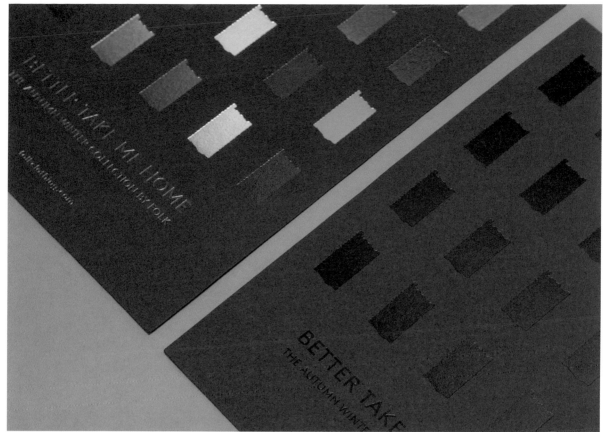

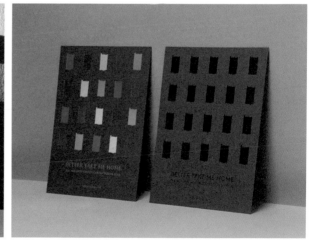

FOLK AW14 PRESS INVITATION

British ready-to-wear label Folk introduces a strong pattern work on top of their signature sleek and functional aesthetic for AW14 collection. Titled Better Take Me Home, the press invite for both men's and women's show features neat foil blocks based on artwork on key pieces from the collections while alluding to windows of a city block, with different palette to represent respective clothing line.

DE: IYA Studio

CL: Folk

PH: Anton Rodriguez

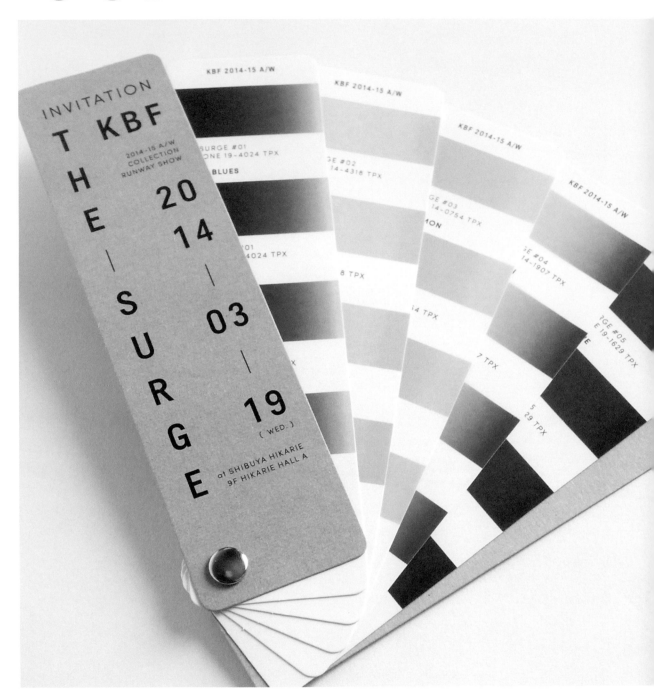

KBF AW14-15 SHOW INVITATION

Japanese label KBF is known for their minimal wardrobe suitable for all modern women. The theme for its AW14-15 collection is "The Surge", which describes a lady's demeanour, and the dynamics of the environment arises around us. With colour gradation being the key visual element of the season, nothing is more appropriate than to present the invitation as a colour swatch book, which when fanned out, showcasing wave of sombre colours.

AD & DE: Hiroe Nakamura

CL: KBF

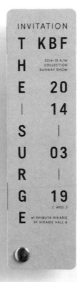

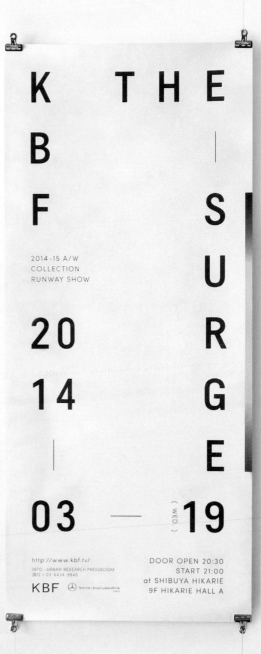

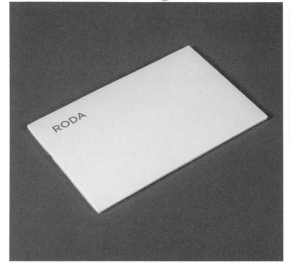

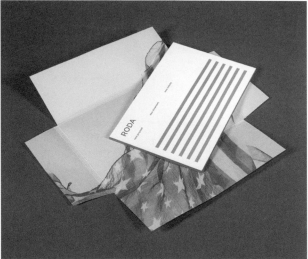

LUCA RODA 2013 SHOWROOM OPENING INVITATION

Invitation for the 2013 showroom opening of Luca Roda is an envelope made from fine paper enclosing a thick cardboard. The envelope is printed on the inside, only reveals itself when unfurled the image of a scarf from the collection to communicate the idea of discovering new creations in the Italian fashion label's new showroom. The card is painted on the edges, suggesting an idea of value and offering a tactile sensation with the material.

DE: Davide Di Gennaro, Pietro Buffa

CL: Luca Roda

PT: Grafiche Mariano

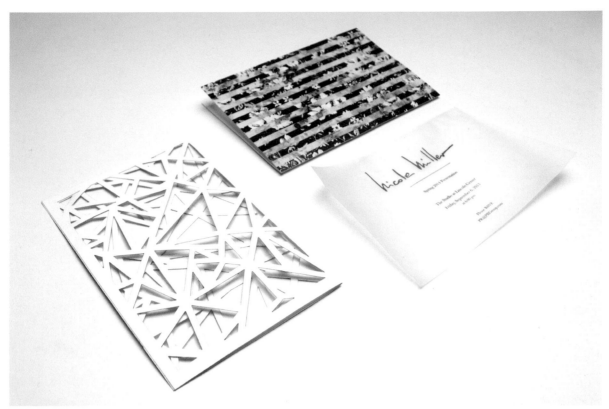

NICOLE MILLER SPRING 2014 SHOW INVITATION CONCEPT

Nicole Miller is a New York-based designer known for her bright prints and patterns. This proposed concept of her Spring 2014 invitation keep her patterns in mind. Comes in a cutout sleeve that mimics the geometric kaleidoscope pattern as seen in the season, details of the show are printed on a translucent paper that separates from the card, so the graphic prints may be reused by the recipient.

DE: Meghan Larimer

CR: Nicole Miller

BASSO & BROOKE 2014 STORE OPENING INVITATION CONCEPT

A student project that envisioned Basso & Brooke's new store opening in Kennsington, where local boutiques and high-end art museums reside. Setting the scene to coincide with the Brazilian and British duo's Spring/Summer release, the set of invitation, event ticket and RSVP adopts bold patterns of the season, then finished with golden envelops and frames to hint exclusiveness.

DE: Paula Peters

THE ESLITE SPECTRUM AW14 MONTHLY BROCHURE & ADVERTISING

The 2014 Autumn/Winter catalogue of Taiwanese lifestyle shopping chain Eslite Spectrum is titled Muse Worship. With reference to fashion magazine covers, a fictional model's portrait is created by collaging images of textile and fabrics from fashion editorials. The image is used as the catalogue cover as well as outdoor advertising.

DE: The Eslite Spectrum Corporation, Meng-Tang Chuang

CL: The Eslite Spectrum Corporation

ANTONIO MARRAS WOMEN'S AW13-14 SHOW INVITATION

Antonio Marras conjures romance and drama with his poetic creations that draw from art, blend cultures and manifesting love for his Sardinian root. His muses for AW13-14 are women of the Bloomsbury Group, an influential collective of British artists and intellectuals active in the early 20th century. Titled with W. H. Auden's namesake anthology, its show invitation is a fold-out book that recreates visits and gatherings where the group enlightened each other.

DE: Studio Paolo Bazzani

CL: Antonio Marras

ANTONIO MARRAS SS14 SHOW INVITATION

Antonio Marras' SS14 show invitation is woodland that comes in a box. Pulling off the rectangle slipcase, a paper doll set opens on four sides and reveals a gloomy fern-filled forest inhabited by a hybrid of sulky girl and reindeer. Aspired to speak about body transformation, Marras expands this otherworldly dimension that draws from Ovid's Metamorphoses onto runway.

DE: Studio Paolo Bazzani

CL: Antonio Marras

THE PILE OF PHOTOGRAPHS DISPLAYING DESIGNERS' NEW COLLECTION DOES NOT HAVE TO BE A PHOTOCOPY OF THE CREATION. PAPER, COLOUR, TYPOGRAPHY, PRINTING AND IMAGE EDITING CAN ALL BE THE MEDIUM TO TRANSFER THE ESSENCE AND THE THOUGHTFUL IDEAS BEHIND THE COLLECTION INTO THE 2D PRESENTATION. AS WHEN FASHION SPEAKS WITH TEXTURE, COLOURS AND FOLDS, SO DO THE HUMBLE PAGES. IT'S CONCERTED EFFORT BETWEEN STYLISTS, PHOTOGRAPHER AND GRAPHIC DESIGNERS, AND IT GOES TOGETHER WITH INVITATIONS AND THE BRAND IDENTITY.

FROM **LOOK** TO **BOOK**

RICK OWENS WOMEN'S SS14 LOOKBOOK

As vicious and proud as they were taking the lead on step dancing through Rick Owens' SS14 Paris runway show, members of the U.S. sorority groups continue to make statement in fearless front-facing portraits in the lookbook. In a 20-paged compilation of images handpicked by the fashion designer himself, the lookbook not only reinforces design but rather makes statement about Owens' ever-rebellious endeavour to work against norms in fashion.

DE: Notter + Vigne

CL: Rick Owens

RICK OWENS MEN'S SS15 LOOKBOOK

The scene where the goat-human masturbate with a nymph's scarf in
Vaslav Nijinsky's controversial Ballet Afternoon of a Faun gets Rick Owens
thinking about primal urge against sophistication, thus his SS15 collection.
Embroideries on the show pieces are based on drawings a young artist Benoit
Taupin left in his house during his stay. The originals are featured in the
lookbook, with Taupin himself modelling the pieces.

DE: Notter + Vigne

CL: Rick Owens

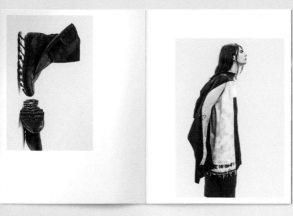

RICK OWENS LILIES 2012 LOOKBOOK

Launched in 2005, Rick Owens Lilies is a diffusion line and pair-down rendition of its glamourously grunge main line. The ready-to-wear collection continues a sombre palette and intricate layering in 2012, which is elaborated by the lookbook. A seemingly elemental layout is put together from uncoated, coated and super gloss paper stock, with trimmed pages to showcase the figure-skimming dresses and draped daywear in optic and textural marvel.

DE: Non-Format

CL: Rick Owens

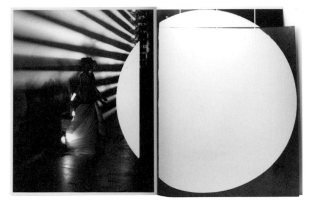

RICK OWENS SS12 LOOKBOOK

Rick Owens' SS12 lookbook captures model's dramatic runway entrance through the "gateway to heaven", as the Paris-based designer calls it. The publication includes pages of varying heights and widths that depict the collection being delineated on stage by a wall of mighty light. Occasionally segmented by wax-coated kraft, some spreads are also overprinted with a dense hit of white ink that imitates the cross section of light.

DE: Non-Format

CL: Rick Owens

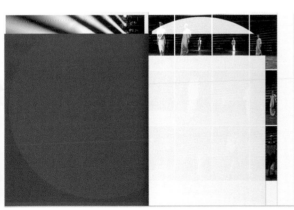

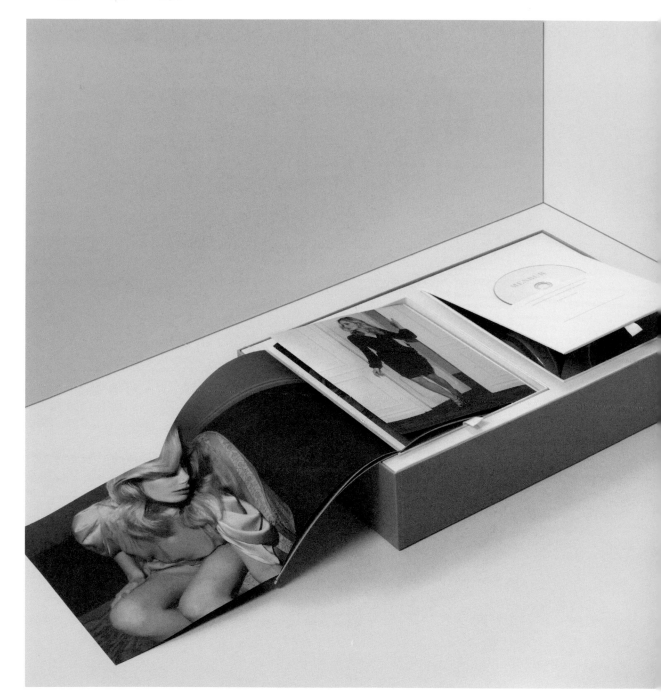

MENBUR A MONOLOGUE OF A DREAM 2010 LOOKBOOK

Creative direction of short film A Monologue of a Dream for the global launch of Spanish footwear and accessories label Menbur. The concept is to transcribe brand experience through a poetic monologue about observations and sentiments of a wearer. A catalogue is made capturing sensual still shots of the debut collection in folding spreads. It is part of the box set made for the short film's presentation, enclosed with a DVD and a sample of the product.

DE: Play&Type

CL: Menbur

CR: Jordi Cussó (FM & PD), Borja López (Photo direction), Monica Zafra (ST)

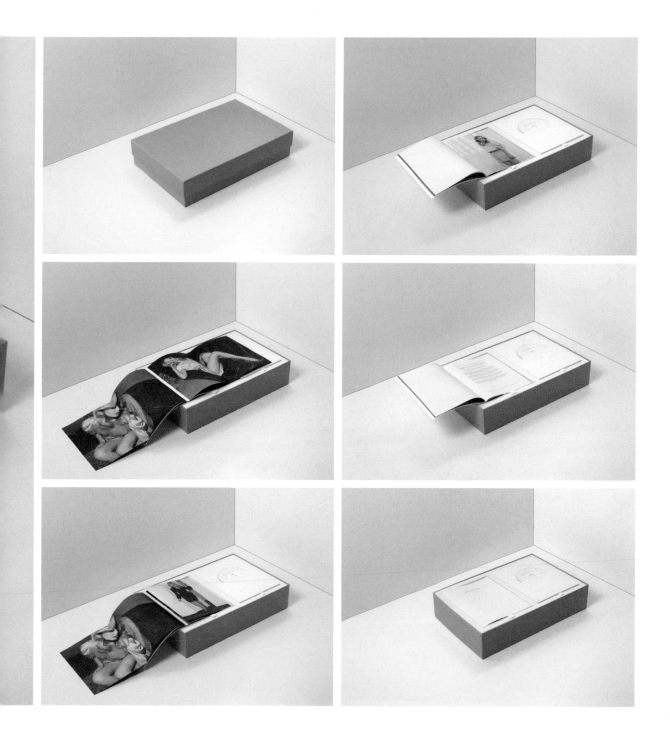

COMPANY & CO SS14 LOOKBOOK

Company & Co offers essential ready-to-wear items that put emphases on comfortable shapes, beautiful fabrics and trendy design. Its SS14 styling shots feature sunshine and country road in line with the collection's chic everyday aesthetic, set off by a light turquoise to keep it cool during the titled Endless Summer.

DE: Play&Type

CL: World Fashion Team

PH: Richard Jensen

SAGE AND IVY SS13 LOOKBOOK

Established by Dutch designer Alexia van Engelen, Sage and Ivy's SS13 collection is all about "RÊVE" (dream). This dream is romantic meets futuristic, constructed through an experimental use of fabrics. The season's lookbook features a doodle of holographic spectrum over the cover girl's eyes that represents her deepest dreams and fantasies. Logotype of "RÊVE" in slender configuration suspenses separately around her to reinforce the theme.

DE: Occult Studio

CL: Sage and Ivy

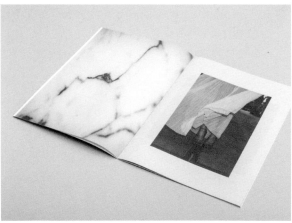

SAGE AND IVY AW13 LOOKBOOK

Sage and Ivy's AW13 collection is themed Melancholia. Responsible for the concept, art direction and graphic design for its lookbook, Occult Studio decks its pages with marble texture, framing the cover in black to set the mood of deep sombreness while backgrounding styling shots in white to set off the showcasing items. The lookbook also includes snapshots that zoom in on notable design details.

DE: Occult Studio

CL: Sage and Ivy

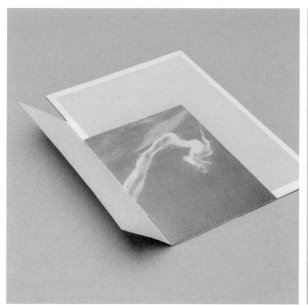

SAGE AND IVY SS12 LOOKBOOK

Sage and Ivy designs women's ready-to-wear that celebrates femininity
as well as social and eco-responsibility. Titled Hemisphere, the label's SS12
collection is themed around water which consists of more than 71% of earth's
surface. The season's lookbook decks runway images with water-based
images from NASA together with soft coloured duotone gradients that create
a misty illusion.

DE: Occult Studio

CL: Sage and Ivy

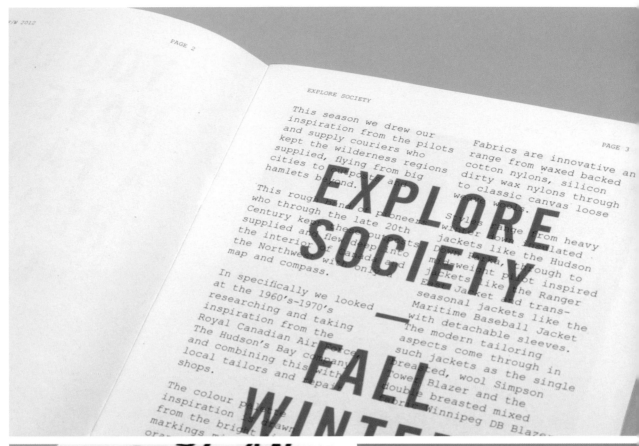

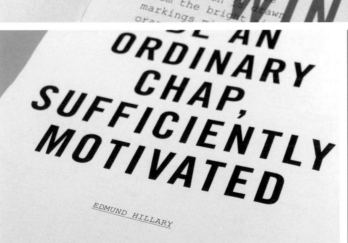

JACK FLYNN FW12 LOOKBOOK

A young Dutch label that focuses on men's tailored outerwear and designed jackets. Jack Flynn's 2012 Fall/Winter collection presents pilot-inspired detailing and palette of arctic rich navy, aircraft aged taupe and bright orange. The season's tailored fit is emphasised in lookbook by styling jackets on outfitter's mannequin. A positive fine is exerted throughout by explorers' quotes that extend full page.

DE: M35, Martijn Tamboer

CL: Jack Flynn

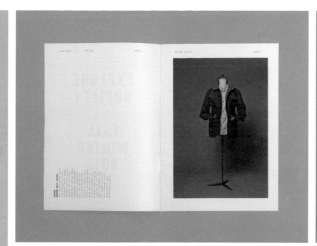

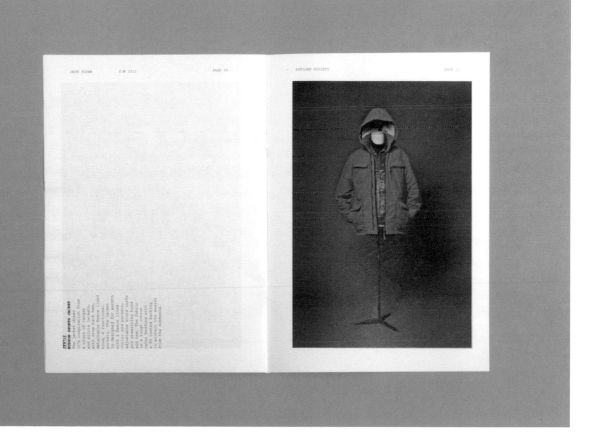

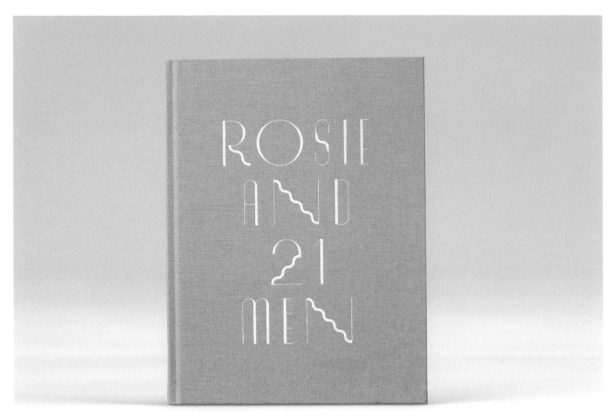

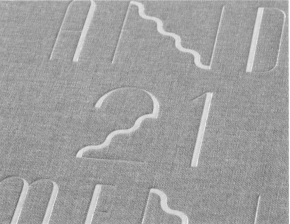

SØLVE SUNDSBØ'S ROSIE & 21 MEN EXHIBITION CATALOGUE

Rosie & 21 Men is the first solo show of Norwegian photographer Sølve Sundsbø in his home country. Curated by Greger Ulf Nilson, the show is held at Shoot Gallery in Oslo. 500 copies of limited edition exhibition catalogue was produced for the event. Chimed in by a slender custom typeface, the pages showcase Sundsbø's work alongside his conversation with British fashion writer Murray Healy.

AD & DE: Non-Format

CL: Shoot Gallery

PH: Sølve Sundsbø

SUPREME MODELS SS11 SHOW KIT

New York-based model agency Supreme Management delivers a composed fresh look for their runway stars as well as the label itself. Their show kit prepared for 2011 global Spring/Summer fashion weeks is a classy black and white box set of well-edited cards, which can be lifted out effortlessly with a pull of the soft satin ribbon. Topped with a silver emboss logotype card stock, the model's styling images are printed in monochrome in elevated elegance.

DE: ceft and company new york

CL: Supreme Model Management

PT: Earth enterprises

SOPHIA LIE

SUPREME MANAGEMENT   TEL +1 212 966-3940   FAX +1 212 966-9614   WWW.SUPREMEMANAGEMENT.COM
199 LAFAYETTE STREET   SEVENTH FLOOR   NEW YORK   NEW YORK 10012

HEIGHT: 5' 11''   EYES: BLUE   BUST: 34''   HIPS: 34''
HAIR: BLONDE   DRESS: 2   WAIST: 25''   SHOES: 9½

AMANDA NORGAARD

JACQUELYN JABLONSKI

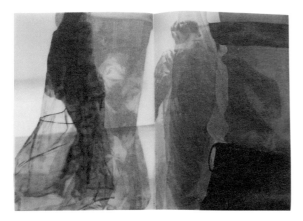

DRIES VAN NOTEN SS13 ANNOUNCEMENT CARD

A 12-page booklet was put together to announce Dries Van Noten's SS13 collection. Compiled from translucent pergamin paper to showcase the collection's chiffon tops and floral sheers with a double-sided silver foil leaf inserted for an announcement, this publication resonates the theme of opacity verses translucency prominent in both the season's collections mesmerised by Dries Van Noten's forte of layering fabrics.

DE: Jelle Jespers

CL: Dries Van Noten

PH: First View, Some/Things(AB), Bache Jespers, Marion LeFlour, Patrice Stable (Fashion shot), Ann Vallé (Product shot)

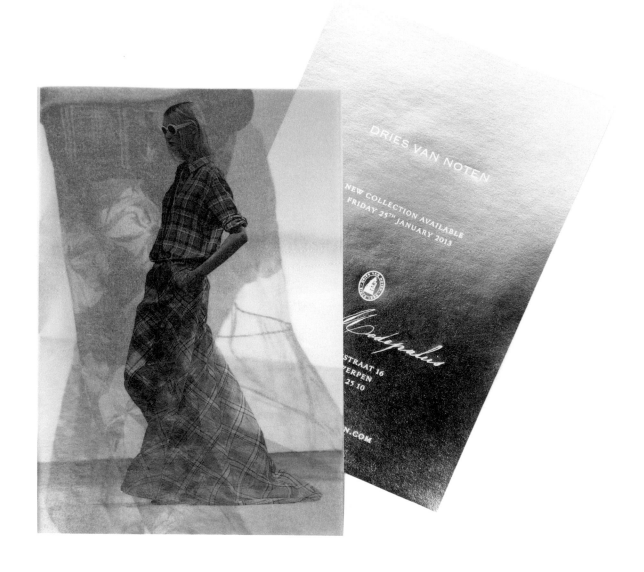

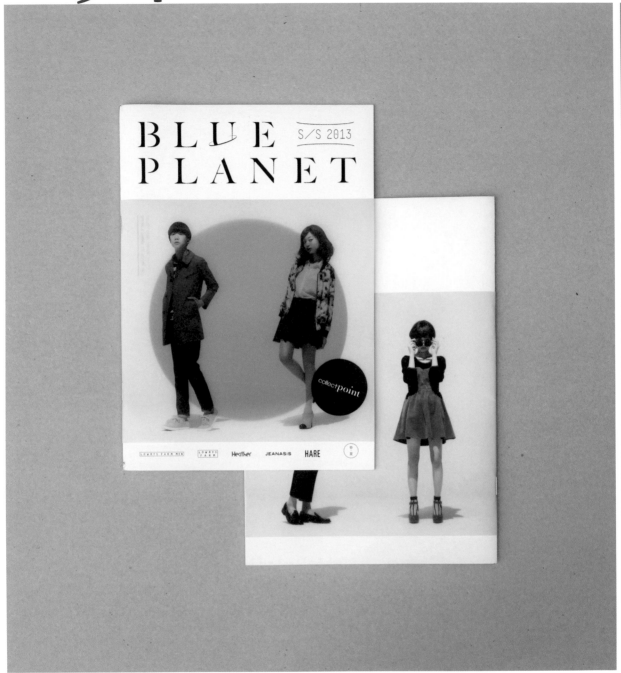

COLLECT POINT SS13 LOOKBOOK

2013 Spring/Summer catalogue for Japan's multi-label store collect point is themed around Blue Planet. The cover in white is simply occupied by a circle in teal, on which a translucent page of styling shot is attached to add layers and blue shades to keep it cool during summer. The concept of space and shape is explored in the styling shots, responded by uneven page dimensions.

DE: THINGSIDID

CL: collect point

CR: collect point japan (PH), Kwuny Wong (CP)

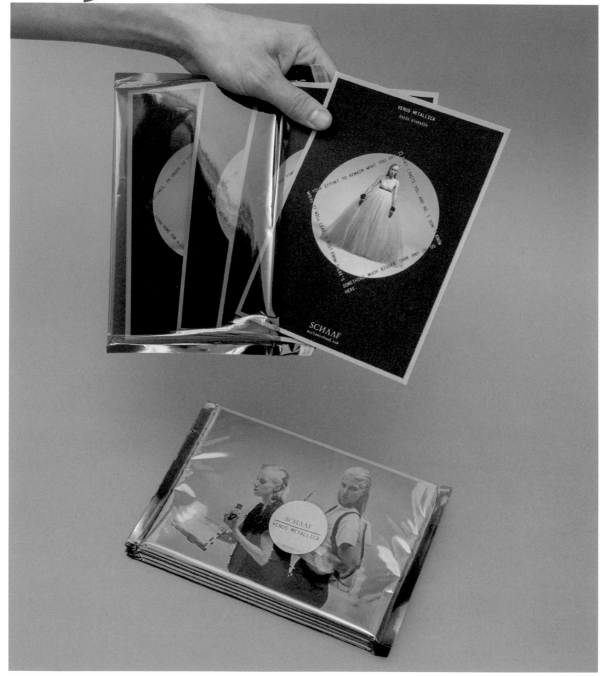

SCHAAF SS13 LOOKBOOK

Schaaf is the eponymous label of fashion designer Miriam Schaaf. The Munich-based brand creates everyday wear with avant garde influence dated back to its earlier years. Its SS13 collection illustrates the life of fictional character Venus Metallica, who lives in a green house in the post-apocalyptic world. Consisting of 16 looks of Metallica in outlandish digital imagery, the lookbook comes in a packet of cards wrapped in silver translucent plastic bags for a futuristic aura likened to the collection.

DE: Moritz Welker, Tobias Knipf

CL: Schaaf

CR: Maret Loopalu, Alescha Birkenholz (Fashion Shot), Yves Krier (Product Shot), Miriam Schaaf, Markus Seer (ST)

VENUS METALLICA

SILK-TOP RETINA
SKIRT WAVE

AND WE FOLLOWED THE RIVER AND WE FOLLOWED THE ROAD AND WE WALKED THROUGH THIS LAND AND WE CALLED IT A HOME BUT HE WANTED THE SUN AND I WANTED THE WHOLE AND THE WHITE LIGHT SCATTERS AND THE SUN SETS LOW

SCИΛΛF
miriamschaaf.com

ISETAN KIDS VACATION STYLE SUMMER 2014 LOOKBOOK

Isetan is a time-honoured department store in Japan. Their Shinjuku flagship carries kids fashion, and two contrary themes namely Marine and Mountain is set for summer 2014. Two catalogues in symmetric covers are designed to connect respective themes, with styling shots of kids mimicking aquatic and outdoor activities. While the layout is reversely identical, the catalogues can be differentiate by bright contrasting hues.

AD & DE: Hiroe Nakamura

CL: Isetan Shinjuku

CR: Yuhki Yamamoto (PH), Hitomi Miyao (ED), Kaori Kawakami (ST), Naoyuki Ohgimoto (MA & HA)

KBF+ SS14 LOOKBOOK

The theme for KBF+'s 2014 SS Collection is Playing Lady. Atypical to their signature minimal style, KBF+ allows feminine floral prints and summer colours for the season that send forth an air of cheerful sophistication. Punning on "play", the collection's lookbook is made into a set of trading cards with 10 characters in various lady power levels. Players can play three games using the card set while browsing different lady styles.

AD & DE: Hiroe Nakamura

CL: KBF+

CR: Kiyotaka Hatanaka @takahashi office (PH), Masaya Umiyama (ED), Nao Koyabu (CO), Natsumi Narita (MA), Roku Roppongi @white STOUT (HA)

BERLIN@M4MODELS.DE
WWW.M4MODELS.DE

M4 MODELS GMBH
T +49 30 616606-6

M4
Madelene

GRÖSSE *178* OBERWEITE *84*
TAILLE *60* HÜFTE *87*
SCHUHE *39*
HAARE *DUNKELBLOND*
AUGEN *GRÜN*

HEIGHT *5'10"* BUST *33*
WAIST *23.5* HIPS *34.5*
SHOES *8.5 US*
HAIR *DARK BLONDE*
EYES *GREEN*

BERLIN@M4MODELS.DE
WWW.M4MODELS.DE

M4 MODELS GMBH
T +49 30 616606-6

M4
Sarah Batt

GRÖSSE *180* OBERWEITE *82*
TAILLE *62* HÜFTE *90*
SCHUHE *41* HAARE *SCHWARZ*
AUGEN *DUNKELBRAUN*

HEIGHT *5'11"* BUST *32.5*
WAIST *24.5* HIPS *35.5*
SHOES *9.5 US* HAIR *DARK*
EYES *DARK BROWN*

M4 2012 SHOWCARDS

M4 is a German model management agency with offices in Berlin and Hamburg. Their sed card set for the year of 2012 endeavours a kaleidoscopic approach, which appears to reflect multi-faceted beauty of their models. In either monochrome or flourish of brilliant colours, the visually arresting deck of cards is difficult to be overlooked.

DE: Eps51 graphic design studio

CL: M4 Models

M4
Dovile Pet

GRÖSSE 177 OBERWEITE 83	HEIGHT 5'10" BUST 32.5
TAILLE 60 HÜFTE 90	WAIST 23.5 HIPS 35.5
SCHUHE 40.5	SHOES 9.5 US
HAARE DUNKELBLOND	HAIR DARK BLONDE
AUGEN GRAU GRÜN	EYES GREY GREEN

M4
Lena Fishman

GRÖSSE 179 OBERWEITE 83	HEIGHT 5'10.5" BUST 32.5
TAILLE 60 HÜFTE 89	WAIST 23.5 HIPS 35
SCHUHE 39 HAARE BLOND	SHOES 8.5 US HAIR BLONDE
AUGEN BRAUN	EYES BROWN

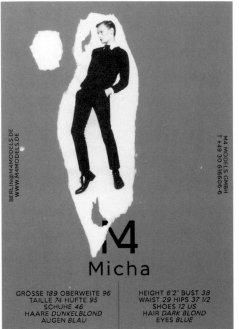

BERLIN@M4MODELS.DE
WWW.M4MODELS.DE

M4 MODELS GMBH
T +49 30 616606-6

M4
Micha

GRÖSSE *189* OBERWEITE *96* TAILLE *74* HÜFTE *95* SCHUHE *46* HAARE *DUNKELBLOND* AUGEN *BLAU*	HEIGHT *6'2"* BUST *38* WAIST *29* HIPS *37 1/2* SHOES *12 US* HAIR *DARK BLOND* EYES *BLUE*

BERLIN@M4MODELS.DE
WWW.M4MODELS.DE

M4 MODELS GMBH
T +49 30 616606-6

M4
Katerina Smutok

GRÖSSE *180* OBERWEITE *81* TAILLE *58* HÜFTE *89* SCHUHE *39.5* HAARE *BRAUN* AUGEN *GRÜN*	HEIGHT *5'11"* BUST *32* WAIST *23* HIPS *35* SHOES *9 US* HAIR *BROWN* EYES *GREEN*

M4 2013 SHOWCARDS

2013 Sed cards design for German model agency M4 is a sophisticated version of a fan's scrapbook. As if slovenly hand-torn from magazine pages, silhouette of models in black and white are friskily put together on cards of versatile washed-out hues. Model information are kept in a similar layout as the previous year.

DE: Eps51 graphic design studio

CL: M4 Models

M4
Anna Nevala

GRÖSSE 176 OBERWEITE 79	HEIGHT 5'9.5" BUST 31
TAILLE 58 HÜFTE 88	WAIST 22 HIPS 34.5
SCHUHE 39	SHOES 8.5 US
HAARE DUNKEL BRAUN	HAIR DARK BROWN
AUGEN BRAUN	EYES BROWN

M4
Isa

GRÖSSE 178 OBERWEITE 76	HEIGHT 5'10" BUST 30
TAILLE 58 HÜFTE 89	WAIST 23 HIPS 35
SCHUHE 39	SHOES 8.5 US
HAARE BLOND	HAIR BLONDE
AUGEN BLAU	EYES BLUE

M4
Jone

GRÖSSE 178 OBERWEITE 84	HEIGHT 5'10" BUST 33
TAILLE 61 HÜFTE 89	WAIST 24 HIPS 35
SCHUHE 39	SHOES 8 US
HAARE BLOND	HAIR BLONDE
AUGEN BLAU	EYES BLUE

M4
Pawel

GRÖSSE 187 OBERWEITE 93	HEIGHT 6'1.5" BUST 36.5
TAILLE 75 HÜFTE 96	WAIST 29.5 HIPS 38
SCHUHE 46	SHOES 12 US
HAARE BRAUN	HAIR BROWN
AUGEN BRAUN	EYES BROWN

M4
Jakob Christian

GRÖSSE 188 OBERWEITE 94	HEIGHT 6'2" BUST 37
TAILLE 77 HÜFTE 94	WAIST 30.5 HIPS 37
SCHUHE 44	SHOES 10.5 US
HAARE DUNKELBLOND	HAIR DARK BLOND
AUGEN BLAU	EYES BLUE

GRÖSSE **177** OBERWEITE **81**
TAILLE **61** HÜFTE **90**
SCHUHE **39** HAARE **BRAUN**
AUGEN **BLAU-GRAU**

HEIGHT **5´9.5"** BUST **32**
WAIST **24** HIPS **35.5**
SHOES **8.5 US** HAIR **BROWN**
EYES **BLUE-GREY**

M4 2014 SHOWCARDS

M4's 2014 sed-card design forges a play on positive and negative space with
velvet colours. Contrasting hues running along tear strip patterns fabricate
a lavishly eclectic background that frames up model's styling shots. Rich
colours in turn accentuate texture of the images in greyscale.

DE: Eps51 graphic design studio

CL: M4 Models

M4

Corinna

GRÖSSE 180 OBERWEITE 87   HEIGHT 5'11" BUST 34.5
TAILLE 62 HÜFTE 90   WAIST 24.5 HIPS 35.5
SCHUHE 39 HAARE BLOND   SHOES 8.5 US HAIR BROWN
AUGEN BLAU   EYES BLUE

M4

Lena

GRÖSSE 178 OBERWEITE 84   HEIGHT 5'10.5" BUST 33
TAILLE 62 HÜFTE 89   WAIST 24.5 HIPS 55
SCHUHE 39 HAARE BLOND   SHOES 8.5 US HAIR BLONDE
AUGEN BRAUN GRÜN   EYES BROWN GREEN

DIRECT

M4

Ella Kandyba

GRÖSSE 178 OBERWEITE 84   HEIGHT 5'10" BUST 33
TAILLE 56 HÜFTE 89   WAIST 23 HIPS 55
SCHUHE 39 HAARE BRAUN   SHOES 8.5 US HAIR BROWN
AUGEN BLAU   EYES BLUE

DIRECT

M4

Elza

GRÖSSE 178 OBERWEITE 84   HEIGHT 5'10.5" BUST 33
TAILLE 60 HÜFTE 89   WAIST 23.5 HIPS 56
SCHUHE 39 HAARE BRAUN   SHOES 8.5 US HAIR BROWN
AUGEN GRÜN   EYES GREEN

ALI SHARAF 2014 PROMOTIONAL MAILER

Based in Bahrain, Ali Sharaf is fashion, beauty and lifestyle photographer. As part of his new brand identity, Sharaf's portfolio is compiled into an A5 promotional mailer. The photographer's selected work in separate cards to allow tailored inserts into a concrete grey duplexed folder, all having identical die-cut tabs and is held in place with a black elasticated band. Marked by a sans-serif logotype, this restrained layout helps to set off details of his work.

DE: Mash Creative

CL: Ali Sharaf Photography

Makeup: Leila Nasser | Hair: Waheeda Rawnaq

Shaima Al Mansoori | 2014

Makeup: Nadiaalblushi Makeup

Alia Dashti | 2013

Makeup: Ala Beauty Aalon

Makeup: Azhar Hubali | Hair: Waheeda Rawnaq

Paper Girl, Harayer Magazine | 2012

Makeup: Nadiaalblushi Makeup

It's About Making An Image, Tonne Goodman | 2013

Makeup: Waheeda

2014

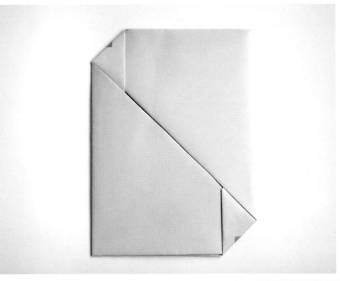

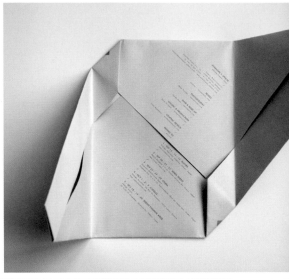

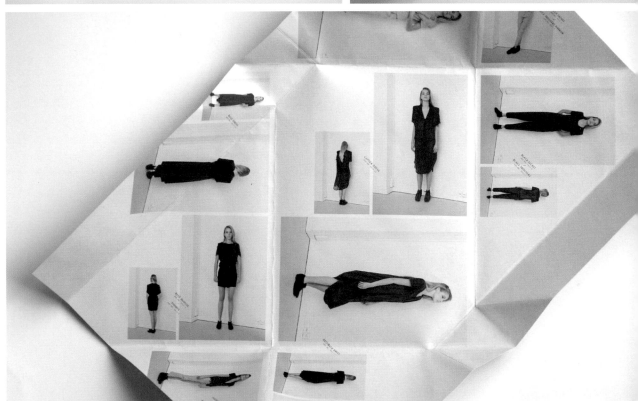

PENELOPE'S SPHERE SS12 POSTER

Penelope's Sphere is a Berlin-based label that creates eclectic womenswear
defined by rugged curves, draping and sombre palette. Mastermind behind
the label is designer Tamari Nikoleishvili, whose idea for SS12 is a feminine
and refreshing look. The season's looks are condensed into a single sheet.
A classic and secured note fold forms a nice frame for the cover image, while
unfolding unveils a tangram of style shots.

DE: Studio Hausherr

BEIGE JACKET

BEIGE TROUSERS

BLUE JA

BEIGE TROUSERS

PENELOPE'S SPHERE

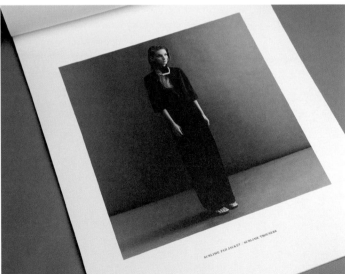

ALICE FINE AW13 LOOKBOOK

Alice Fine believes in a diverse fashion world. The Swedish fashion label is keen on collaborating with other creative fields and exerts its artistic flair with nonconformist concepts. Meticulous yet easy to wear, their AW13 collection oozes exclusive elegance as before, and is captured in a 40-page hanger lookbook. The limited edition of 500 are hanged brimful on custom made copper racks on display at Stockholm Fashion Week as an installation in itself.

DE: Snøhetta

CL: Alice Fine

PH: Anders Lindén @Agent Bauer, Erik Five Gunnerud

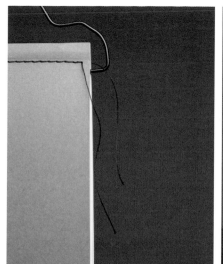

ALICE FINE

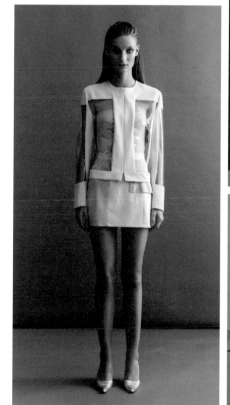

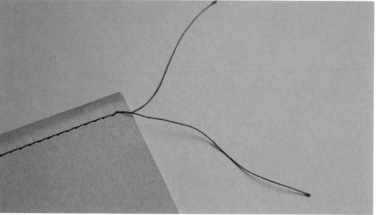

HUDSON SHOES MAIN LINE LOOKBOOK

Established in 1990, Hudson is a British footwear label famed for their signature play on androgynous looks and innovative craftsmanship of leathers. Their mainline for the season is inspired by the sharp tailoring of Savile Row in the 1960s and iconic films such as The Graduate. Showcased in separate postcards, the set is encased in a bespoke grey cardboard wallet with handmade leather fastening.

DE: IYA Studio

CL: Hudson

PH: Anton Rodriguez

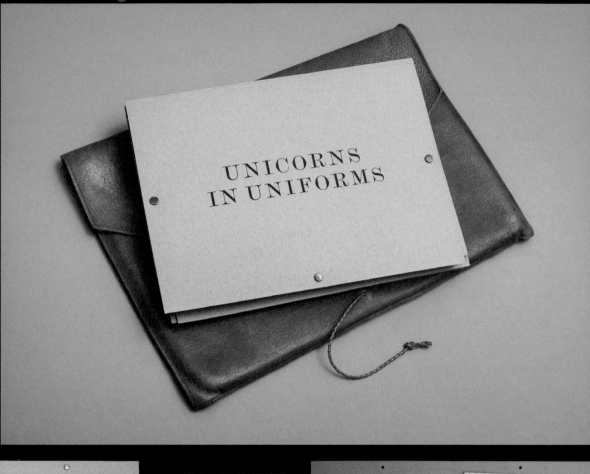

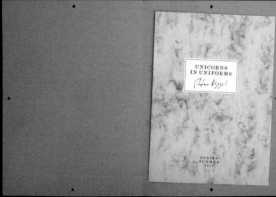

STEFANIE BIGGEL SS13 LOOKBOOK

Titled Unicorns in Uniforms, Stefanie Biggel's SS13 collection epitomises

DE: Bureau Collective

Stefanie Biggel   Autumn Winter   13

I leave you my portrait

I leave you my portrait

STEFANIE BIGGEL SS14 LOOKBOOK

Stefanie Biggel is a fashion designer from Zurich. Her namesake label's SS14 collection asks "If you ever need a stranger". It's a story of anonymity and loneliness told through juxtaposed fabrics like neoprene and tulle as well as urban-inspired prints showcased in the lookbook by two girls whose gazes never meet. Fastened in a kraft board folder, words are printed in white to be lighthearted for the season but secluded to show desertion.

DE: Bureau Collective

AMI PARIS SS13 LOOKBOOK

AMI is a men's ready-to-wear label founded by Alexandre Mattiussi in Paris. Easy, chic and charm, the label is defined by the designer as a "proposition of real clothes for a real man". Its SS13 collection sends forth relaxed country spirit with soft tailoring, earthy tones and a bespoke Bird's Pattern by Violaine & Jérémy. This lead pattern, drawn by hand with colour pencils, also decks an elongated lookbook that catalogues the collection outfit by outfit.

DE: Violaine & Jérémy

CL: AMI Paris

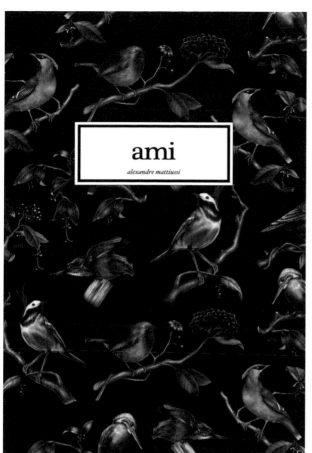

ACNE STUDIOS SS14 LOOKBOOK CONCEPT

Acne Studios creates ready-to-wear defined by founder Jonny Johansson's juxtaposing designs. As her personal project, Illustrator Rosalie Kate Whittingham creates a lookbook for the Stockholm fashion house's nautical inspired Spring/Summer 2014 collection. A bright, contrasting palette is used in her painted depiction of the season's items to reflect playfulness and sleek style presence in previous lookbooks and campaigns.

DE: Rosalie Kate Whittingham

CR: Acne Studios

Acne

SPRING / SUMMER

2014

L O O K S

1  *2* *3*

6  *7*

4 *5* *8* *9* *10*

STORES

AMSTERDAM
Oude Spiegelstraat 8
Amsterdam, The Netherlands
amsterdam@acnestudios.com
+31 20 4226845

ANTWERP STORE
Lombardenvest 42
Antwerp, Belgium
antwerp@acnestudios.com
+32 32 25 05 22

BERGEN STORE
Christiegate 9
5015 Bergen, Norway
bergen@acnestudios.com
+47 55 32 32 55

BERLIN
Münzstrasse
10178 Berlin, Germany
berlinshop@acnestudios.com
+49 3028 044870

COPENHAGEN
Pilestræde 40
Copenhagen, Denmark
pilestrade@acnestudios.com
+45 33 93 00 90

GOTHENBURG
Magasinsgatan 19
411 18 Gothenburg
Sweden
magasinsgatan@acnestudios.com
+46 31 13 85 80

HAMBURG
Bleichenbrücke
20354 Hamburg, Germany
hamburg@acnestudios.com
+49 40 69607533

LONDON
13 Dover Street
London w1s4ln, uk
doverstreet@acnestudios.com
+44 20 7609 9374

MELBOURNE
502 Melbourne 300
350 Bourke Street
Melbourne vic 3000
Australia
300@acnestudios.com.au
+61 3 9650 0201

NEW YORK
33 Greene Street
New York 10013, usa
greenestreet@acnestudios.com
+1 212 334 8345

OSAKA
1-9-8, Shinsaibashisuji, Chuo-Ku,
542-0085,
Osaka, Japan
osaka@acnestudios.com
+81 66258870

OSLO
Grønnegata 1
0350 Oslo, Norway
gronnegata@acnestudios.com
+47 22 59 45 00

PARIS
1 Quai Voltaire
75007 Paris, France
quaivoltaire@acnestudios.com
+33 1 42 60 51 88

SEOUL
Shinsegae Main Store
5f, 52-50 Chungmuro 1ga
Jung-gu, Seoul, South Korea
sagmain@acnestudios.com
+82-2-2026-9000

SHANGHAI
Shop 212, Reel Department Store
no. 1601 Nanjing Road West
Shanghai, China
shanghaireel@acnestudios.com

STAVANGER
Breigata 8
4006 Stavanger
Norway
stavanger@acnestudios.com
+47 51 55 85 16

STOCKHOLM
Norrmalmstorg 2
111 46 Stockholm, Sweden
norrmalmstorg@acnestudios.com
+46 8 611 64 11

SYDNEY
28 Glenmore Road
Paddington
Sydney, Australia
paddington@acnestudios.com.au
+61 2 9360 0294

TOKYO
5-3-20 Minami-Aoyama
Minato-Ku Tokyo, Japan
aoyama@acnestudios.com
+81 3 6418 9923

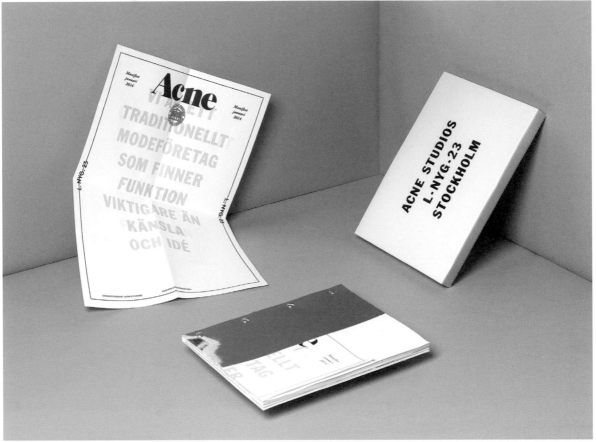

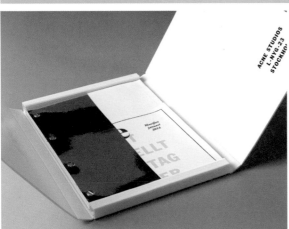

ACNE STUDIOS PROMOTIONAL BOOK & POSTER CONCEPT

As a student project, Therese Ottem was asked to produced a promotional book and poster for a brand of her own choice. Her pick is Swedish fashion house Acne Studios. Bright hues, robust typography as well as an amalgam of page dimensions, materials and folds manifest the label's refusal to be defined. The intentional use of Swedish is a homage to Acne's origin while differentiate it from fellow brands in the designated American market.

DE & PH: Therese Ottem

PH: Acne Studios (Fashion shot), Peter Kanai (Product shot)

VI BRYR

OSS INTE OM

NORMATIVA

RAMAR

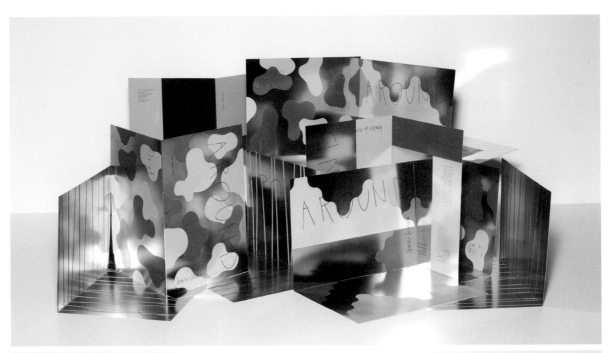

L'ATELIER DU SAVON AW14 CATALOGUE

Brochure for the Autumn/Winter 2014 collection of Japanese fashion label l'atelier du savon is a magic mirror set made from paper. The season's theme is "View around you", a call for customers to choose their wardrobe according to the view they see that day. Brimming with kaleidoscopic patches of yellow, lime, blue and brown, coated card stock in silver are folded in two, with the season's styling shot on the inside.

AD & DE: Naonori Yago

CL: AMBIDEX

CR: Kazuhiro Fujita (PH), Katsuro Okunuki @amana inc. (PD), art factory (PT), Michio Hayashi (ST), Hiromi Chinone (MA & HA)

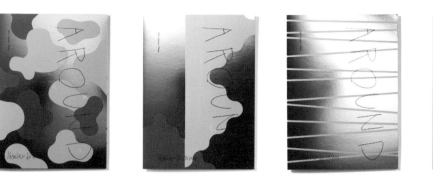

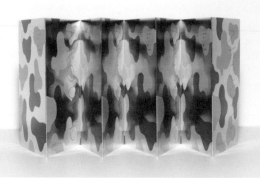
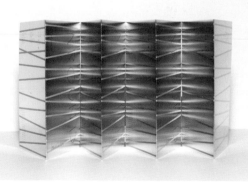

MOBEL SPORT 2013-14 CATALOGUE

Customised sport and team wear with the latest technology, a Spanish label Mobel regard innovation as their very core value. A series of catalogues are created to showcase eight of their product lines. Illustrated by photography, infographics and minimum text, each condenses garment design for a given sport. Washed-out covers are decked with tailored icons on robust-coloured booklets that attach from the outside.

AD & DE: Sublima Comunicación, Rubio & del Amo

CL: Mobel Sport

CR: Mariano Fiore (AD & DE), Mario Miranda (PH)

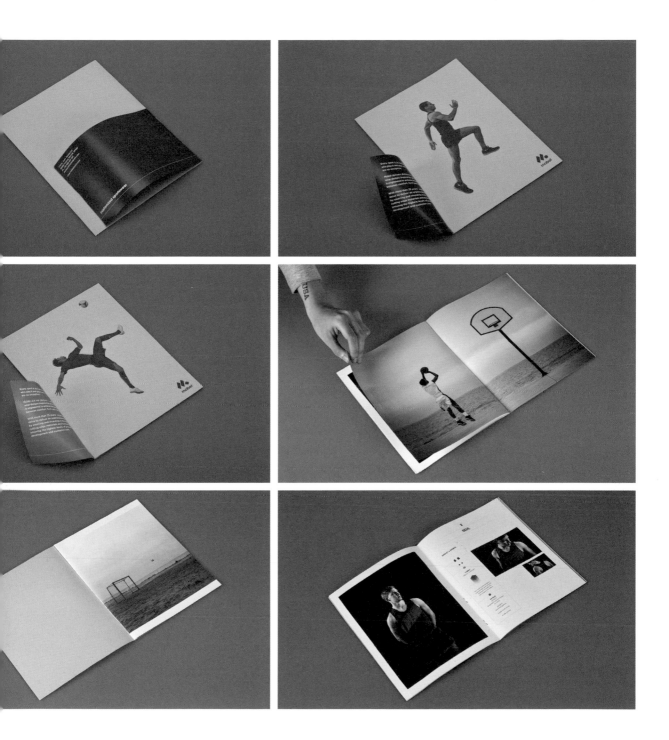

HEAD SS14 LOOKBOOK

Head is a sportswear label specialising in tennis-related sportswear and equipment. Its SS14 lookbook comes in a washed out cover but surprises readers with contrasting colours that categorise product lines, namely Performance and Vision for men, women and children. Graphic design is drawn from the sport itself, where perpendicular lines, shapes and rich hues of tennis courts are deconstructed and used to visually enrich the lookbook.

DE: Two Times Elliott

CL: Head International

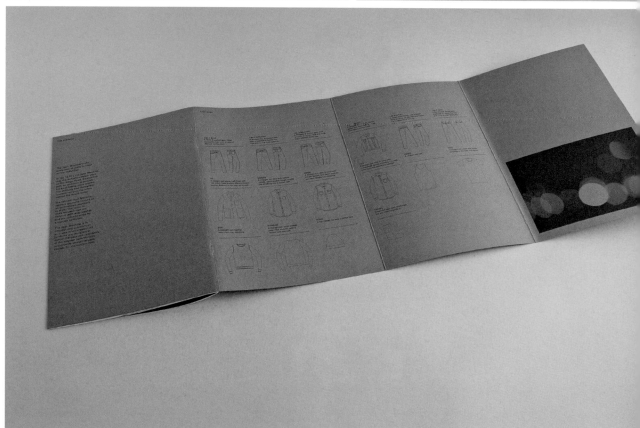

JEAN.MACHINE AW13 LOOKBOOK

Jean Machine was the UK's definitive denim store in the 1970s. The label is revived in 2013 as "Jean.Machine", a premium men's denim line designed to deliver the ease and confidence of the original Jean Machine brand. The revived label's AW13 lookbook features modelling shots that manifest its understated approach to style. The moss green cover can be unfold to reveal Jean.Machine's design range and unique cuts.

DE: Two Times Elliott

CL: Jean Machine

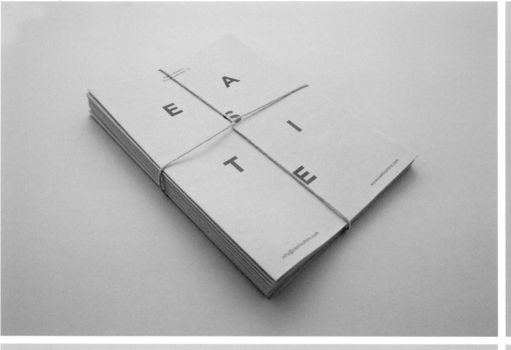

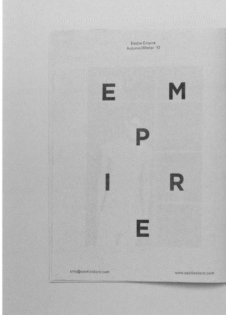

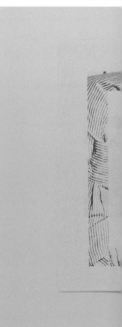

EASTIE EMPIRE AW12 LOOKBOOK

Eastie Empire Tailors is a sports heritage clothing label based in London. Sourcing fabric from time-honoured British mills, it styles tailored vintage clothing with modern functionality and comfort. The label's AW12 lookbook is Risograph-printed in blue, showcasing items with light and shadow. Each of their design is named after a real life or imaginary gentleman, whose name is scribbled on the styling shot as well as embroidered onto the garment.

DE: Two Times Elliott

CL: Sara Weston

We're all about the combination of press and stitching, as you find so often in heritage sportswear.

This tuxedo style is inspired by a Victorian rowing top, constructed in heavyweight drill mixed with canvas for added warmth just like the original.

Press & Media

Sona Communications
Ben Art-Grove
ben@sonacommunications.com

Maria Polo
maria@sonacommunications.com

Buyers & Wholesale

Selmid Agents
Rob Pawloy
rob@linearmargins.com

Sales & Enquiries

Eastie Empire
Dave Weston
sale@eastieclass.com

Design

The Paley Effect
tony@allodious.co.uk
hello@allodious.co.uk

We salute clothes with character that tell a story. We are a British sports heritage label, combining all the good traditions of tailoring with bespoke vintage style fabrics. Our alliance with long established British mills is key to generating the standard of fabric we require. Reviving old manufacturing techniques to deliver authenticity and style with substance.

Our inspiration comes from vintage sportsmen east and west, adventurers and gentlemen. We find this inspiration in antiques markets, archive photo libraries, auctions, vintage fairs, museums and art galleries.

With each piece we imagine the type of man who would have worn it and stitch his name as an embroidered name tag into each garment. However, our vision is not to dress men like Victorian gentlemen. We temper this with modern day styling, functionality and comfort. Bringing the two worlds together.

The recipe for each Eastie piece is tailoring ingenuity, charm via little details and revived fabrics. We believe, like good old fashioned sportsmen that 'Manners Maketh Man'.

Our 1044 pea coat is inspired by heritage college sports wear, with waterproof panels big enough for honest, torn toggles and classic herringbone tape.

MENBUR YOU INSPIRE ME PHILOSOPHY BOOK

Wrapped in pink synthetic leather with satin ribbon bookmarks, Menbur's 2012 Brand Book would be easily mistaken as a girl's personal diary. This intended design is to play down the label's corporative manner. In the chapter You Inspire Me, Menbur narrates in first person its creative process with illustrations. The spirit of the brand is also delivered within letters, in the photo album to keep the story-telling as intimate as possible.

DE: Play&Type

CL: Menbur

IL: Veronica Ballart Lilja

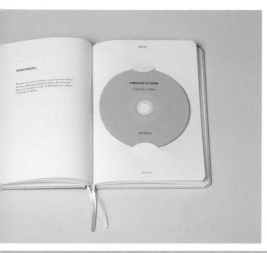

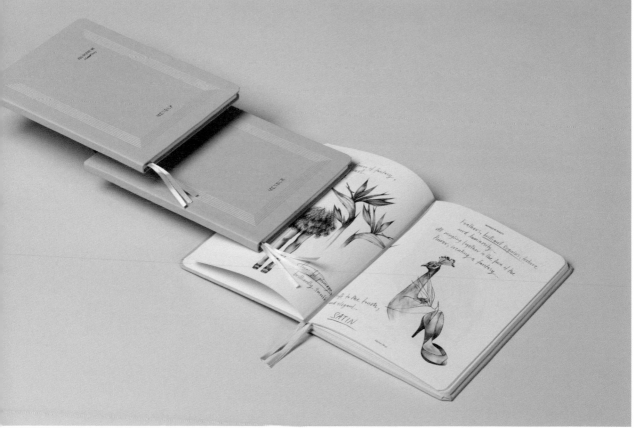

HONOR 2013 BRAND BOOK

Honor's womenswear translates the nostalgia of an old-world atelier into something sophisticated, wearable and modern. Simple and refined, a custom suitcase is crafted to encase the Spring and Fall brand books that tell the Honor story in 2013. Wrapped in ornate covers reflective of the two seasons' signature patterns and palettes, the editorial compile both runway and studio shots to convey feminine aesthetic unique to the brand.

DE: RoAndCo

CL: Honor

SPRING
2013

FALL
2013

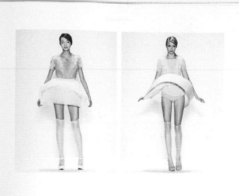

RETAILERS, LABELS, COLLECTIONS, SHOWS — ALL NEEDS SOMETHING TO SOLIDIFY BRAND CONCEPTS. IT'S NOT JUST ABOUT THE NAME AND A CORPORATE FACE, BUT A TOTAL PACKAGING THAT REPRESENTS THE GENERAL ATTITUDE. WHILE RETAILERS AND LABELS FOCUS ON BEING MEMORABLE, IDENTITIES FOR SHOWS AND COLLECTIONS CREATE ANTICIPATION AND EXCITEMENT. FROM A BRILLIANT LOGO TO ART DIRECTIONS FOR PHOTO-SHOOTING, THIS SECTION SHOWCASES THE ESSENTIAL ELEMENTS THAT HELP BRANDS IDENTIFY THEMSELVES AGAINST THE OTHERS.

FROM **BRAND** TO **IDENTITY**

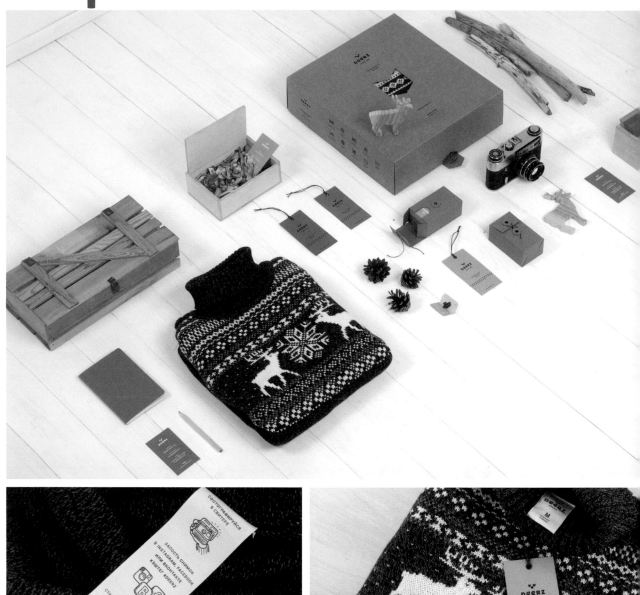

DEERZ REBRANDING

The 30-year-old Russian online store has been reborn anew, with a minimal logotype, glue-free packaging box and a hearty laundry symbol set. Featuring a graphical deer's head and an angular lettering, the logo mark allows flexible application and underlines knitwear and Scandinavian designs as Deerz' key products. An earthy palette completes the corporate image with emphases on its use of natural materials and quality.

DE: Eskimo Design Studio

CL: Deerz

CR: Anatoly Vasiliev (PH),
F61 Work Room (PT)

DEERZ

SINCE 1984

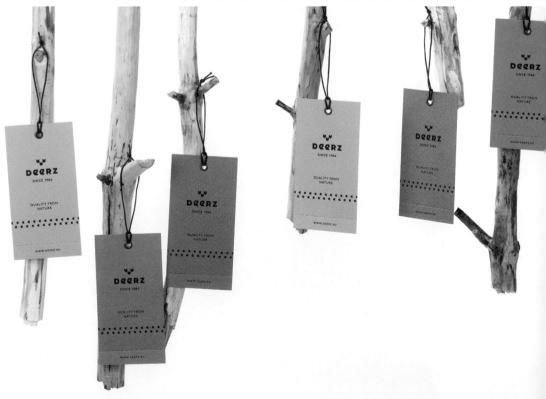

I LOVE SHOES BRANDING

I Love Shoes' new logo design talks directly to shoe-lovers. Knowing what it takes is good to cherish their shoes, Eskimo devised a changeable logo that can hold the shoe store's name in manifold ways; and serve as a real shelf that made to display goods, shoe care products and stationery in store. The white, yellow and brown palette was meant to create the feeling of comfort and easiness with flair.

DE: Eskimo Design Studio

CL: I LOVE SHOES

DE: Anatoly Vasiliev (PH),
F61 Work Room (PT)

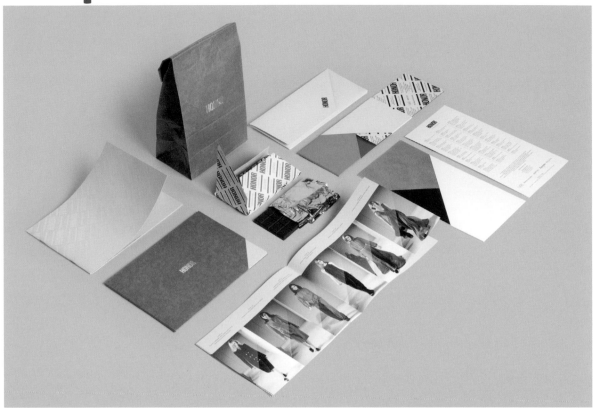

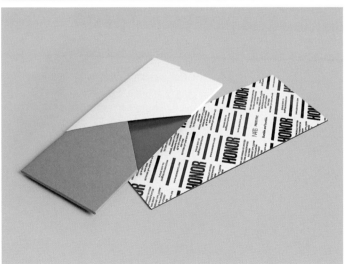

HONOR FW11 IDENTITY

Honor's designer had drawn on her childhood memories to create the Fall collection. The idea about finding beauty in the mundane surroundings was extended to the season's lookbook and invitation, with lavish gold foil and high-gloss spot-varnish contrasting ordinary cardboards and kraft-paper sleeves. Diagonal folds and cuts subtly revealed the collection's signature emerald colour, while large chocolate bars bearing the brand's logo gave a nostalgic hint.

DE: RoAndCo

CL: Honor

CR: Gerardo Somoza (Runway shot), Fine & Raw (Custom chocolate)

CANDELA BRANDING

Gabriela Perezutti, the designer behind Candela, draws partly on her childhood on an Uruguayan horse range to create her footwear and ready-to-wear clothing. A swooping gold logo and lush leather packaging were introduced to acknowledge her South American roots. A decorative script sets off the gaucho spirit with a soft femininity that prevails the line.

DE: RoAndCo

CL: Candela

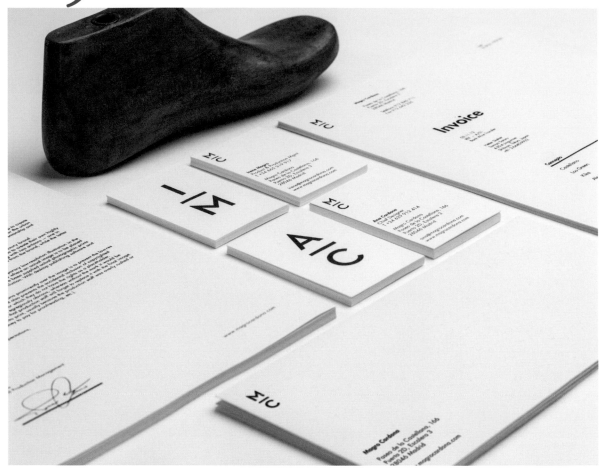

MAGRO CARDONA BRANDING

Magro Cardona is a Madrid-based women's footwear brand founded by Irene Magro and Ana Cardona. The brand's designs are produced in the traditional shoe factories of Toledo by experienced craftsmen. Their emphasis on time-honoured traditions, craft and vanguard is translated through three logo versions. The pared-down stationery layout and gold stamp on packaging also reflect refinement in details.

DE: Mark Brooks Graphik Design

CL: Magro Cardona

PH: Jorge de Bobadilla (Fashion shot), Sandra Gallardo (Product shot)

MAGRO
CARDONA
MADE IN SPAIN

M|C

Founded in Madrid, 2012

Magro Cardona employs time-honored techniques of Spanish craftsmanship to create shoes that balance a touch of the rebel with minimalist classicism. Inspired by and created for the urban woman, Magro Cardona's shoes reinvent the classics with a focus on quality, expert craftsmanship and attention to detail.

Irene and Ana -- Magro & Cardona -- met in 2009 while working for the same luxury brand. They were drawn together by a common vision of style and decided to join forces to create their own highly personal brand. Irene and Ana live and work in Madrid and are collaborating with two artisans -- one in Alicante and the other in Toledo. The former focuses on the feminine designs from the brand, while the latter works on the masculine.

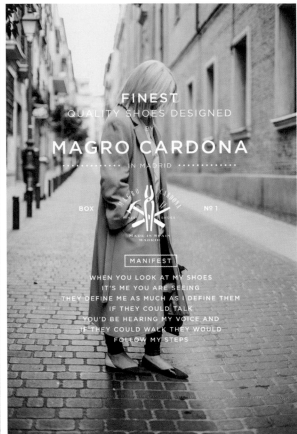

FINEST
QUALITY SHOES DESIGNED
BY
MAGRO CARDONA
• • • IN MADRID • • •

BOX   Nº 1

MANIFEST

WHEN YOU LOOK AT MY SHOES
IT'S ME YOU ARE SEEING
THEY DEFINE ME AS MUCH AS I DEFINE THEM
IF THEY COULD TALK
YOU'D BE HEARING MY VOICE AND
IF THEY COULD WALK THEY WOULD
FOLLOW MY STEPS

MAGRO CARDONA

Nº 9

Magro Cardona
F/W 2014 Collection
Season Lookbook — #9

MADRID + TOKYO
LONDON + NEW YORK
COPENHAGEN

Finest Quality Shoes
Made in Spain
magrocardona.com

HAUTE VINTAGE BRANDING

Haute Vintage store's luxury vintage pieces and special designer items never goes out of style. They asked for an identity that can withstand time like its classic stock, and moodley responded with a modern design, using the simpliest colours and a clean typeface. Proportions in design is perfectly executed, from the paper size, to the font, and even the illustration commissioned for the gift card.

DE: moodley brand identity

CL: Haute Vintage

IL: Izabela Arsovska

L U T H I A ® IDENTITY

Argentinian brand Luthia's brand identity is as simple and exquisite as the handmade backpacks and totes they sell. Where the bags' quality unfolds in the slightest details, empatía's attention focused on the paper stock and printing, which features a porous, pure white paper and a subtle, blind embossed logo. A white and grey colour combination elevated the minimalistic approach and created an aesthetically pleasing brand.

DE: empatía®

CL: L U T H I A ®

PH: Brenda Berruti (Product shot)

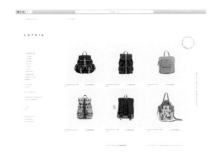

AKIN IDENTITY

AKIN celebrates femininity with clean designs. Where the label encapsulates
its concept in geometric forms and silhouettes, its visual identity translates
it into thickness, visible in its ultra-bold marques and ultra-thick business
cards. The logotype presents an integral guide to everything AKIN. A compact
version of the logo in seal form gives a nod towards the brand's aesthetics.
The bright orange specifically referenced AKIN AW14 collection's palette.

DE: Sam Lane

CL: AKIN

MHL PACKAGING & LOOKBOOK

In many aspects, the sleek, clean packaging designs sum up Margaret Howell's design philosophy that incorporates make, functionality and natural looks. As well as an update of the brand's identity, also designed by StudioSmall, the new approach catches the eye with a large malformed typeface and more evident cues for a handmade appeal. Flexible basic designs also improve functionality of MHL's tapes and clothing labels.

DE: StudioSmall

PH: Aleksi Niemelau

MCKILROY BRANDING

McKILROY curates for confident and stylishly incognito men. The notion of cultivating an air of obscurity in the shop guided the identity, resulting in a range of tactile applications that seem to mask the logomark, conceived with eight typefaces to connote its eclectic offering. The idea was supported by its countdown posters, a lead-up to the message "WE ARE OPEN" as it's removed bit by bit to reveal the storefront.

DE: &Larry

CL: McKILROY

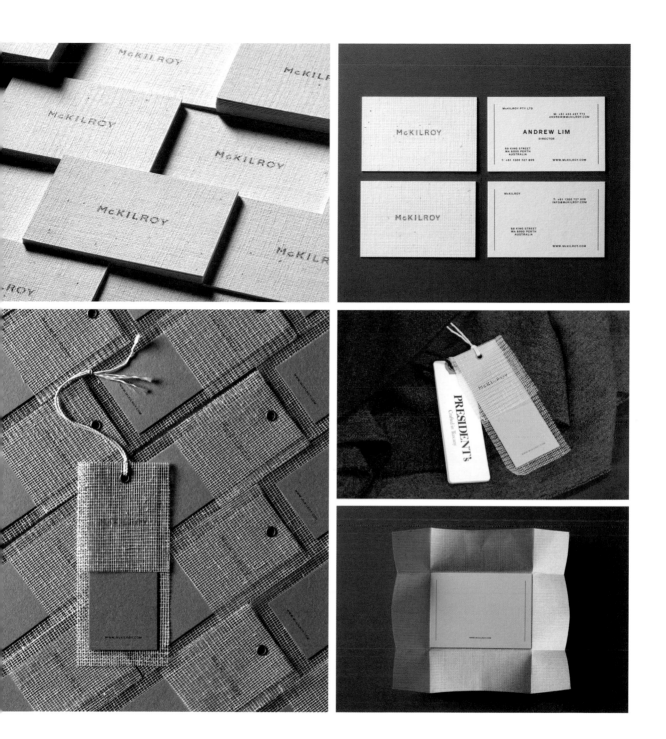

McKILROY

D.J.M. CHILDREN'S FASHION STUDIO IDENTITY & PACKAGING

An illustration-based identity highlights the fine fabrics that make D.J.M.'s clothes charming and sweet. As "comfort, naturalness, and simplicity" are valued by the brand, patterns of these wool and cotton fabrics adorn D.J.M's logo, communications and the catalogue book. The system also sees thoughtful details like garment-shaped stickers and cutouts that enable interactive play. Only recycled paper and cardboard has been used.

DE: Egle Ciuciulkaite

CL: D.J.M. Children's Fashion Studio

ANDREAS KLEIBERG IDENTITY

Whether it's still or moving, Andreas Kleiberg's images often demonstrate a distinct focus on his subjects. This promotional kit introduces the photographer in a similar fashion, with his initial centring on individual items, as a sprayed mark on his tabloid-style portfolio and business card, produced from a recycled paper with a metallic finish and blind debossed frames. The accompanying tote bag also bears a bold, capital blackletter 'A' print.

DE: Bleed (Joakim Jansson, Baptiste Ringot)

CL: Andreas Kleiberg

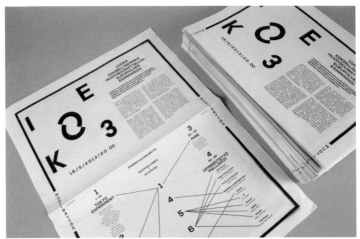

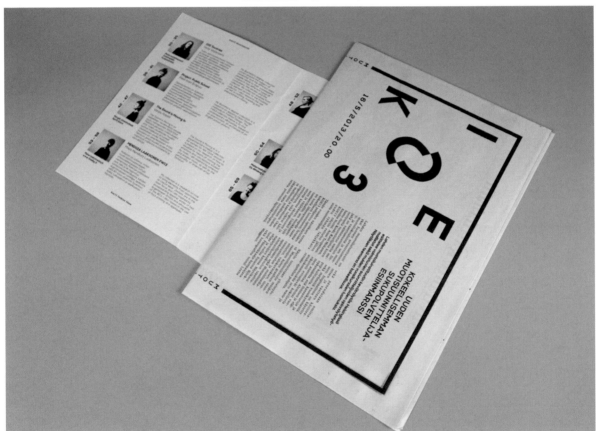

KOE13 FASHION SHOW IDENTITY

The KOE13 fashion show by Lahti Institute of Design was set to present experimental collections created by fashion graduates from various years and grades. While styling for KOE13 Fashion Show was inspired by a fashionable health check, the event's visual identity was founded on a logotype. The slashed and shifted '0' was possibly indicative of breaking cycles and groundbreaking attempts.

DE: Aino-Maria Loviisa Vuoti

CR: Panu Salonen (PH), Minna Cheung @Fashion Design department, Lahti Institute of Design

NAAA TAA BRANDING

Designed by Natasha Trayan, NAAA TAA is a unisex label that creates minimalistic, timeless but also unique one-off clothes. To reflect the design, Evan Dorlot created a minimal visual identity by using black against white and a geometric type. Be amused by the numerous styles of the letter 'A' which manifests itself as acute cuts and modules of the logotype that assemble an 'N'. The individual letters dot around business card and stationery also contribute an airy and playful ambience.

DE: Evan Dorlot

CL: Natasha Trayan

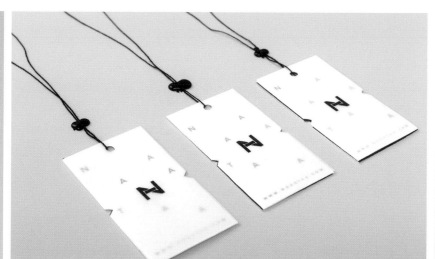

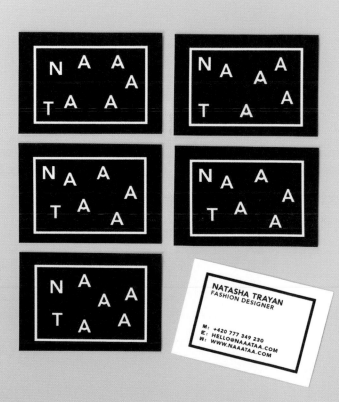

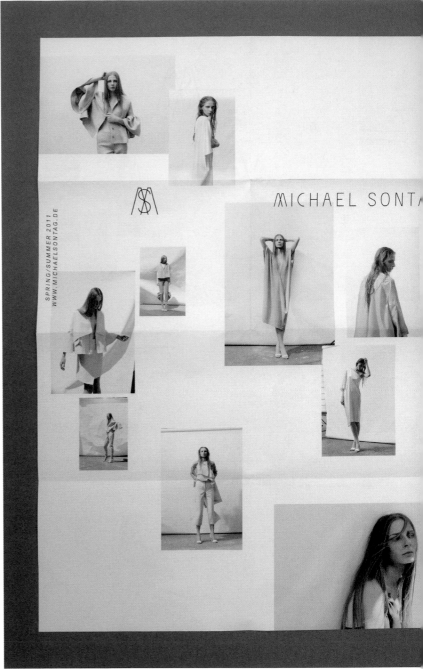

MICHAEL SONTAG 2010-14 IDENTITY

Designer Michael Sontag sees his own work as an entity, so as the way Eps51 perceives the designer's eponymous label. Comprised of individually designed glyphs, MS' logotype endures as a label and an emblematic signet that appears in concert or separately on various touchpoints. Christian Schwarzenberg's atmospheric photography rounds up MS' identity and turns it into a visual entity.

DE: Eps51 graphic design studio

CL: Michael Sontag

PH: Christian Schwarzenberg

MICHAEL SONTAG

GREIFSWALDER STR. 208B
10405 BERLIN
WWW.MICHAELSONTAG.DE

SPRING/SUMMER 2011

AGUA MARINA BRANDING

Agua Marina is a new brand of luxury womenswear. Using a curvaceous
typeface as the key visual, and combining it with monochrome fashion shots
and a understated yellow, the proposed identity sets the tone for the brand's
ethos and celebrates the sophisticated spirit that is Agua Marina woman.
The presence of the fashion designer, in the manner of a signature, suggests
commitment in a personal sense.

DE: Jona Saucedo

LOOK ADDICT BRANDING

Fashion blog and online store Look Addict updates new fashion trends, inspiration and photo shoots from all around the world daily. Its bold brand design very clearly underlines drugs; and making a statement that fashionistas' love for styles is almost like a hardcore drug addition. By using aqua blue and minimal design, the drug and needles do not seem off putting anymore but give out a very clean and chic impression.

DE: Noeeko

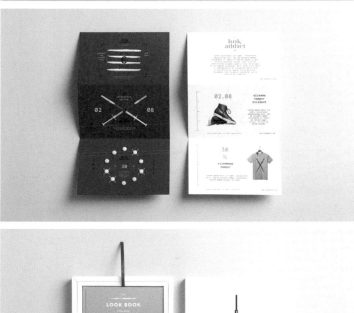

PAGE THREE HUNDRED IDENTITY

Craftsmanship is prioritised throughout Page Three Hundred's fashion and identity design. Just established in 2014, the young, independent label promises all their clothes are designed and handmade in Italy. A bold, modern packaging set accentuate the clear focus on quality, with clean types and huge labels highlighting minor details that actually plays a huge role in defining their apparels. Hand-stamped brand cards recount the label's philosophy in words.

DE: Page Three Hundred

CR: Alberto Raviglione (PH), Eleonora Giammello (ST), Chiara Cima (MA & HA), Elisa Fili (MO)

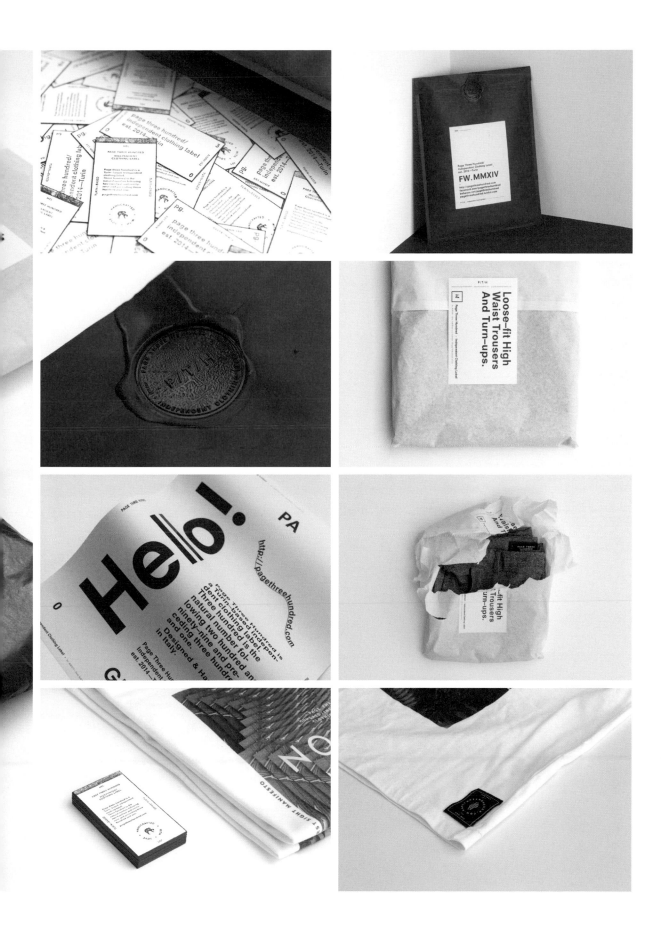

KOMBI REBRANDING

Established in 1961, Kombi is a Montreal-based family brand of winter clothing accessories. A brand overhaul is performed to help rejuvenate its identity. In a distinctive vermilion-led palette to express warmth, a new logo is adopted to emphasise Kombi's care for both the upper and lower body. Packaging and printed communication amongst others are titled with fun and heart-warming narratives about the products and a call for heading outdoors.

DE: Polygraphe

CL: Kombi

CR: Olivier Ricard (CG),
Ellen Teitelbaum (CP)

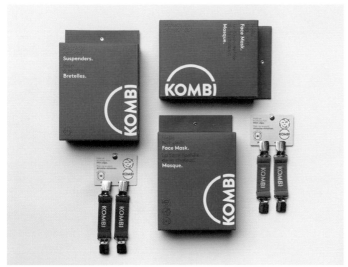

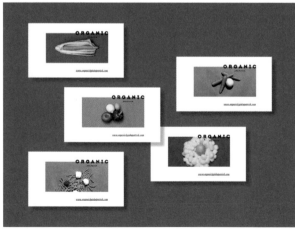

ORGANIC BY JOHN PATRICK FRESH FASHION IDENTITY

Organic by John Patrick's clothing answers to both beauty and ethics. Likened to an organic farm, the brand acquired a visual identity where fresh healthy yields were stylised and photographed in lieu of models and Organic's works. Where fashion items are physically absent, bold colour combinations and surreal proportions bring an edge of fashion through images to Organic's stationery and postcards, and leave no bounds to the imagination.

DE: Tannia & Ahmad

CL: Organic by John Patrick

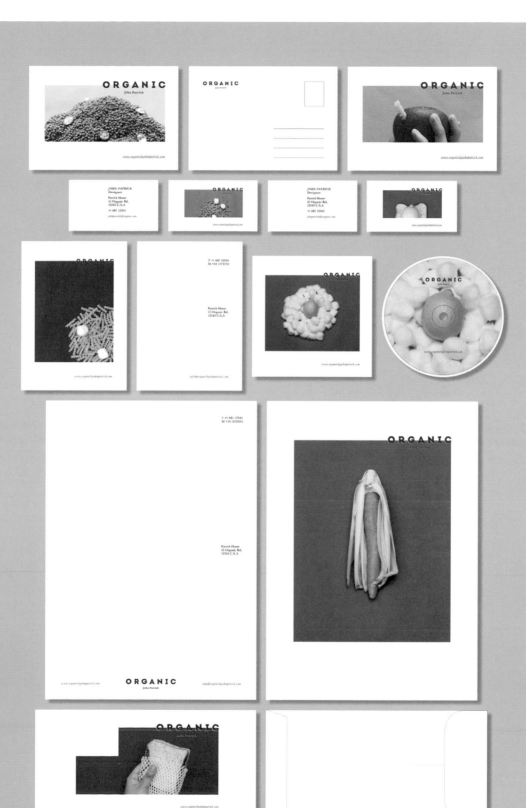

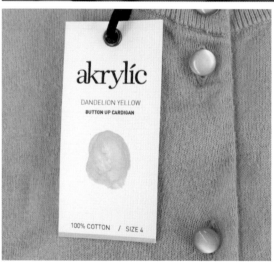

AKRYLIC BRANDING CONCEPT

Shopping at Akrylic is heightened by rainbow hues. Besides its emphases on quality tailoring, Akrylic's products also boast a full colour range which are chromatically organised for young, fashion-conscious urbanites to explore. Centring on its colour element, starting with a name that comes as a variant spelling of acrylic paint, the branding for the shop unites the concept with a themed catalogue, paint-tube packaging, and a paint-blotch style logo.

DE: Lacy Kuhn, Lacey Nagel, Franny Canine

POODLE SKIRT TEE
$30 USD / £20 GBP

PETAL PURPLE TOP
$40 USD / £25 GBP

GRAPE SKIRT
$50 USD / £35 GBP

BLUE RAZZ TOP
$70 USD / £40 GBP

MIXED BERRY JACKET
$70 USD / £40 GBP

FUSHIA BLOUSE
$45 USD / £65 GBP

ROYAL PINK TOP
$40 USD / £30 GBP

CHERRY RED SWEATER
$70 USD / £40 GBP

FLAME SKIRT
$35 USD / £20 GBP

CALICO RED TANK
$40 USD / £25 GBP

FIRE HYDRANT JACKET
$120 USD / £70 GBP

POPSCICLE TROUSERS
$60 USD / £80 GBP

MELON SWEATER
$40 USD / £25 GBP

KRILL TROUSERS
$120 USD / £70 GBP

BABY PINK BLOUSE
$45 USD / £25 GBP

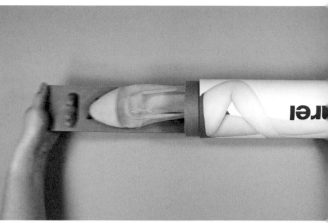

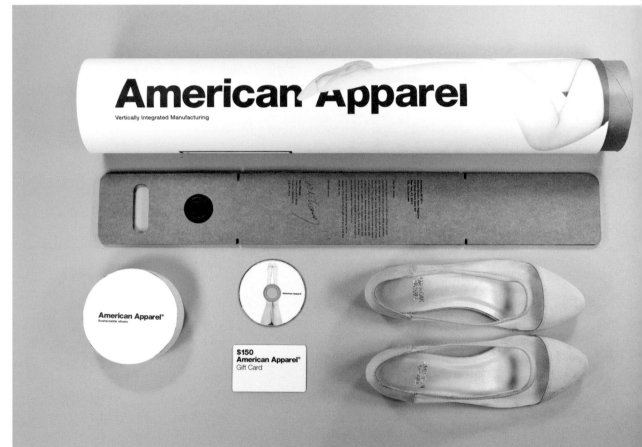

AMERICAN APPAREL PACKAGING CONCEPT

Conceived as a personal project to re-imagine sustainable shoe packaging for American Apparel, the proposal translates the label's "Vertically Integrated Manufacturing" business model into the tube design with an imagery that speaks of the natural beauty of a woman's legs. The packing also stands out for its eco-conscious design. Made from recyclable cardboard, the tube contains a pull-out spine which secures the shoes, gift card and DVD as well as a letter to customers.

DE: Jiajie Roger Wang

CR: Academy of Art University, Dara Weinberg (MO)

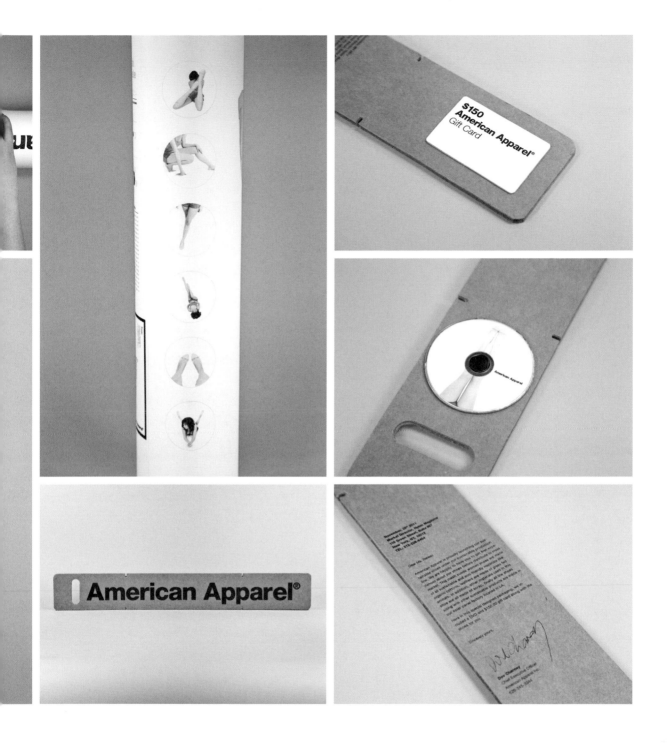

Text visible on packaging:

2014 LIMITED EDITION
NOTE BAG PROJECT

320 × 420
DENIM MATERIAL

13. 01 W /

2014 LIMITED EDITION
WIZWID DIARY PROJECT

× 210

COVER.
GLOSSY SILVER PAPER 80g/m²
UNCOATED CARD BOARD
g/m²

BODY.
UNCOATED PAPER 100g/m²

W/ 2014 NOTE BAG PROJECT

Consisting of a diary in a glossy silver cover and a denim tote bag, the "W/ Note Bag" set was commissioned as complimentary gifts for employees of Korean online shopping mall WIZWID. As a token to encourage efficiency and provide convenience, the products are nonetheless designed and packaged with style. Simple features are spiced up by metallic touch and served as a visual delight to the employees.

DE: mykc, MÜNN

CL: WIZWID

PH: Maeng Min Hwa @MÜNN

2014 LIMITED EDITION
NOTE BAG PROJECT
320 x 420
DENIM MATERIAL
13. 01 W /

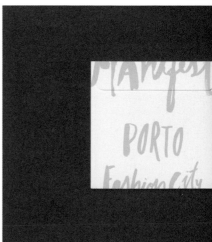

PORTO FASHION MAKERS MANIFEST

A simple square frame makes City Fashion Makers and its city-based affiliates cohere into a knockout brand. As a regional online meeting point for fashion, Porto Fashion Makers represented by an energetic yellow is set to gather what's trending and manifest Porto charm. At the website's launch party, PFM engaged its potential community members with the question "ARE YOU A MAKER?" boldly printed on the event's flyer.

DE: Carla Almeida

CL: Porto Fashion Makers

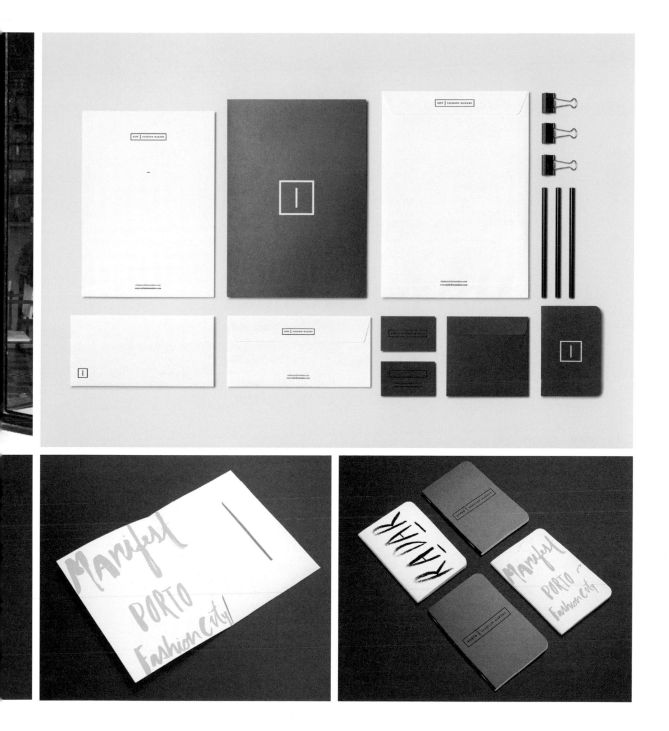

LAFORET 35TH CARNIVAL IDENTITY

The 35th anniversary of the opening of Laforet Harajuku in Tokyo was celebrated in a visual and actual fiesta. On the theme of "Carnival", TYMOTE created a colourful blast at the department store, with mixed patterns and colours illustrative of a "pop, happy world view". The graphic patterns also composed a flexible language for communications, visible in its posters, leaflets and game tickets at the open-air jamboree.

DE: TYMOTE

CL: Laforet Harajuku

SE: KuRoKo inc.

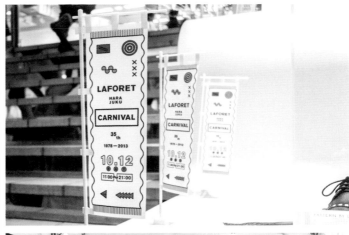

POOLTRADESHOW 2012 IDENTITY

POOLTRADESHOW is a land of opportunities and possibilities for promising young fashion brands. The very idea of uncovering the unexpected and the young spirit were vividly conveyed in a fluid typeface that ran across the event's posters, brochures, tote bags, staff tees and backdrop. The pale azure was the trade show's brand colour, and was used here to stimulate energy and transmit vibe.

DE: Hype Type Studio

CL: Advanstar

PEARLY QUEEN LONDON IDENTITY

Pearly Queen London cites classic 1980s swimwear as a key influence. The brand identity captures the zeitgeist perfectly, with a sprinkle of pearlescent, holographic and iridescent finishes and substrates, a playful logotype, and a bright vivid palette to keep the tone of voice young and spontaneous. Alternate logo appearing as a crown accessories PQL's swimwear and recurs as a print on reusable packaging zip bags.

DE: Passport

CL: Pearly Queen London

SANLO IDENTITY

With chapters in Mexico and the States, Sanlo's founders handpick beautiful jewellery from the most unusual places around the world. The idea of travelling the world runs seamlessly throughout the shop's identity, from postcards of various origins and design details inspired by suitcases, to its monogram comprised of typefaces from different cultures. Apalette directs viewers' attention back to the gems that burst with femininity and sophistication.

DE: Firmalt

CL: Sanlo

A WADDED DREAM PACKAGING & PROMOTION

A Wadded Dream is a Hong Kong-based cotton-wadding handicraft store. Focusing on animals and botanic beauty, the label creates an exquisite dreamscape with cotton. The brand's packaging and collateral are themed around "dream". Besides storage and display, soft cushions are designed as the daydream place for animal accessories.

DE: THINGSIDID

CL: A Wadded Dream

CR: Vanessa Chan (Hand crafter)

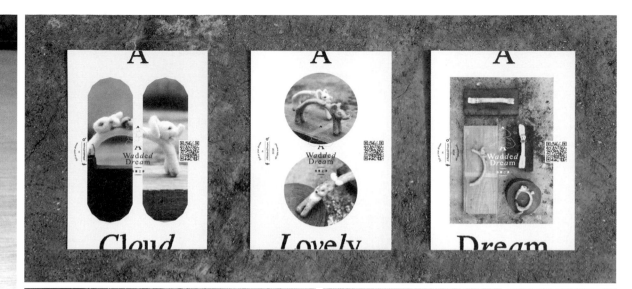

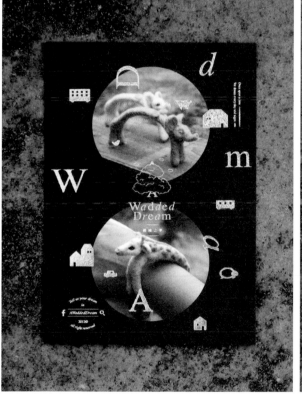

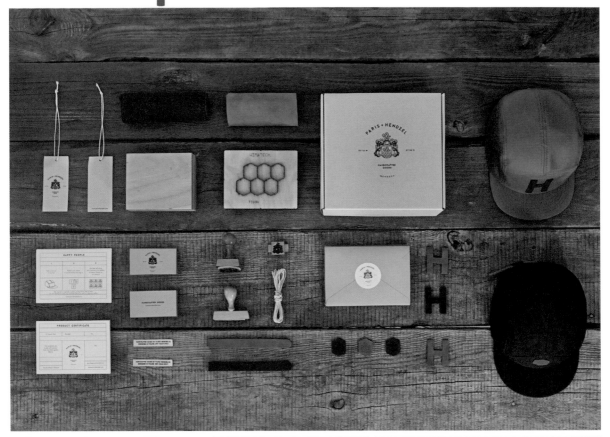

PARIS+HENDZEL HANDCRAFTED GOODS BRANDING

Using Prawdzic, Polish coat of arms as their logo, P+H takes pride in being a noble company. From the making to the final packaging of products, all products are made by hand, and each created with great attention to details. With each order the customer receive a product certificate with customer's own name printed on it, along with product details and its serial number.

DE: Paris+Hendzel Studio

CL: Paris+Hendzel Handcrafted Goods

TEALER IDENTITY

A self-proclaimed "T-shirt dealer" established in 2012, Tealer is a Parisian brand focusing on men's street wear with a quirky edge. A full-blown branding concept is developed for the label, including design of their online shop, street marketing and an extended accessories range of five panel caps, cigarette holders, skateboards, and more. Various logos are tailored for the packaging of each product category, but all united under a robust sports club aesthetic.

DE: Say What Studio

CL: Tealer

CR: Chateau Batârd

PAINTBOX BRANDING

New York manicure studio Paintbox specialises in classic manicures and design-driven nail art. Aligned as two corner brackets, the coral pink foiled paintbox logo keeps nail design in focus across the studio's collateral, campaign and web design. A kaleidoscopic pattern evokes scenes of edgy fashion films and the indulgence of high designs in the campaign.

DE: Lotta Nieminen

CL: Paintbox

PH: Jamie Nelson

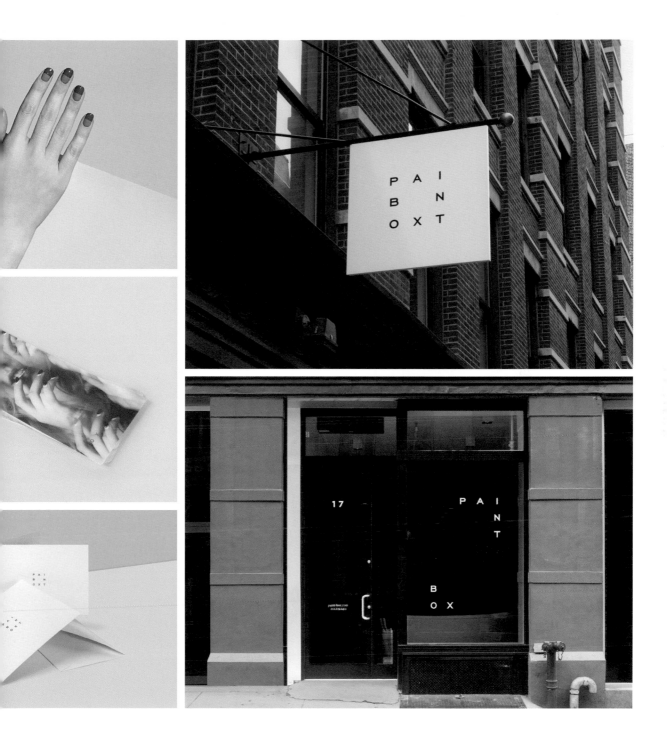

ART IS A MATTER OF TASTE BRANDING

Lisa Brandstaetter's blog speaks to a clique of fashion lovers who hold critical reviews in high regard. A palette and motif comprised of black and rose contribute a nod to femininity, yet project a resolute tone that caters to admiring eyes. A clean and elegant logo completes the brand image with the blog's motto "Art is a Matter of Taste".

DE: Marie Zieger

CL: Lisa Brandstaetter

MARTA BRANDING

Graphic designer Dawid Cmok created a functional and minimalist design for women's urban clothing line Marta. To work with but not against the floral pattern that is frequently used, Marta's logo is playful and not stiff, easily recognisable, yet not forgetful. The solution covers a range of standard and custom-made items, including logotype variants, letterheads, envelopes, visiting cards, folders, patterns, an identity book, and accessories.

DE: Dawid Cmok

CL: Marta

ROKKEBERG CONCEPT STORE BRANDING

Dedicated to urban culture and lifestyle, Rokkeberg serves coffee next to home accessories and its in-house fashion brand. A suite of wayfinding icons was devised to identify the retail zones, and compliment the shop's logo, all united by a basic badge-like frame. A old, pale pink and black evoke the shop's vintage offerings and aesthetics throughout its communications and interior.

DE: Carolin Wanitzek & Dennis Adelmann

CL: Rokkeberg Concept Store

MARKETING PRODUCTS IS NO LONGER ITS SOLE PURPOSE, IT HAS BECOME AN EXHIBITION ITSELF. TIME, SPACE, PRODUCTS — EVEN THE LEAST RELATED OBJECTS CAN BE BROUGHT TOGETHER AND TAKE UP FIGURAL MEANINGS WITHIN CONFINED WINDOW FRAMES. PHOTOGRAPHERS, GRAPHIC DESIGNERS AND MULTIMEDIA CREATIVES TAKE IT TO ANOTHER LEVEL WITH THEIR HANDS-ON KNOWLEDGE AND SPECIAL SKILLS. SPECTATORS PARTICIPATE AS THEY WALK PASS AND INTERACT WITH THESE ELEMENTS. THE RESULTS ARE SIMPLY INSPIRING AND TAKING IMAGINATION FAR BEYOND FASHION PER SE.

FROM WINDOW TO INSTALLATIONS

GUNEE HOMME SS15

Mounted like a sculpture, by abandoning its conventional form as a garment, and by filling in random objects such as broken glass and grid lines, the setting turns GUNEE's menswear into an abstract piece of art, and possession of them into collecting art. A reduced background sets off the label's work that often features striking patterns and playful prints comprised of bold colours and overstated designs.

CD & PH: Madame Peripetie

CL: GUNEE Homme

CR: Emily Pugh (SE), Stella Arion (ST)

GUNEE
HOMME

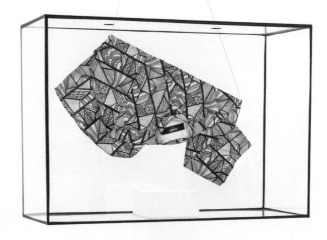

ODESSA SERIES

Printed on a cheap piece of paper are, an expensive jewellery often an evidence of wealth, just next to a vintage brooch from a flea market. The juxtaposition represents merging of Ukrainian kitsch and their contradictory desire to look luxurious. Suspended on a wire side by side, the design exposes the ironic outlook on Ukrainian fashion as the Odessa Series attempts to depict.

CD & PH: Madame Peripetie

CL: Masha Reva x Syndicate of Kiev

CR: Stella Arion (ST), Claudine Blythman (MA), Show Fujimoto (HA), Max @profile (MO)

MASHA REVA X SYNDICATE

ODESSA SERIES

SONIA BY SONIA RYKIEL FW14

An eponymous diffusion line of the designer, Sonia by Sonia Rykiel translates the label's Parisian impertinence into a more colourful and graphic look. Set design for their Fall/Winter 2014 collection fashion film is curtained by walls of flowing pastel stripes. Inspired by Japanese minimalism and vitality, this installation accentuates a free spirit that is prominent in the line's identity, while delivering lighthearted urban sensuality unique to the design.

DE: Bonsoir Paris

CL: Sonia by Sonia Rykiel

CR: Kaname Onoyama (Photo direction), Caporal Films (PD)

HERMÈS MÉTAMORPHOSE SHORT FILM

A social video was created to impart Hermès' Métamorphose campaign into the digital domain. A pink flamingo shaped by high heel laces, a tie disguised as ice lolly — it is a whimsical dimension where everything transforms into something new. Shooting live in a handmade setting, Hermès' Spring/Summer collection comes to live in this tactile and quirky visual narrative.

DE: Vallée Duhamel

CL: Hermès Paris

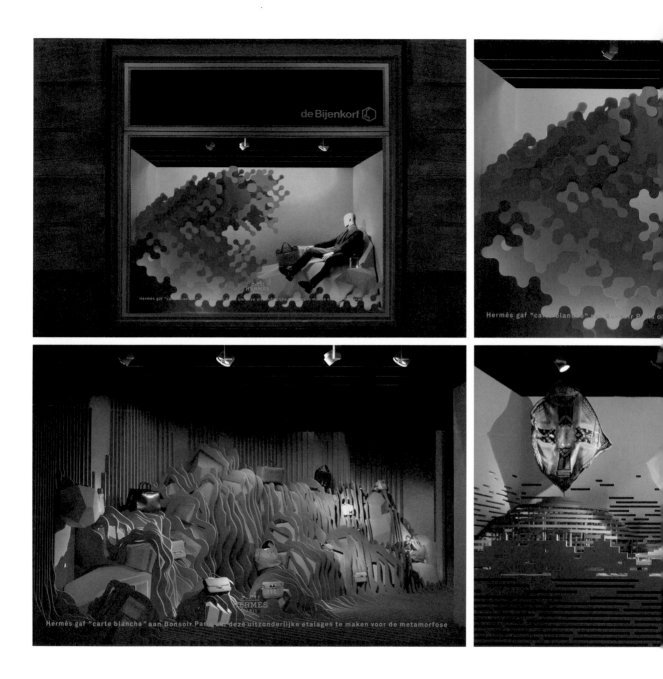

Hermès gaf "carte blanche" aan Bonsoir Paris om deze uitzonderlijke etalages te maken voor de metamorfose

HERMÈS METAMORPHOSIS WINDOW INSTALLATION

Symbolic of its location, water was imaginatively rendered to create a narrative window setting for Hermès at De Bijenkorf department store in Amsterdam. Sculpted out of wood, mix of still and moving pieces formed through CAD modelling and digital milling blended natural and digital aesthetics in layers, with much to absorb when seen in person. Each window depicted water at a different state, from calm water to jets and waterfalls.

DE: Bonsoir Paris

CL: Hermès Paris

CR: Barbara Kieboom (PH),
Cédric Hugonnet (RT),
Brenninkmeijer & Isaacs (PD)

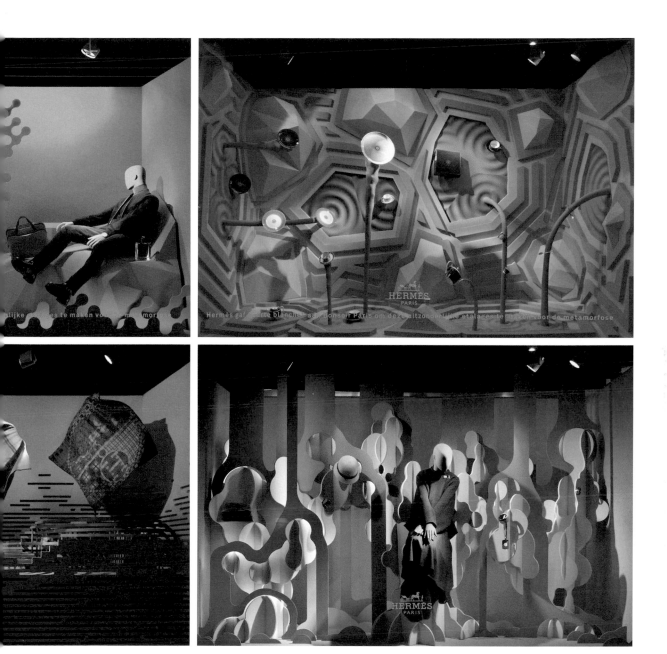

HERMÈS
PARIS

HERMÈS
PARIS

GALERIES LAFAYETTE THE WHITE PAGE

Galeries Lafayette's "Quoi de Neuf" has become, throughout its many seasonal editions, a must-see event for the discovery of new trends in fashion. According the season's concept "The White Page", Bonsoir Paris carefully-tailored 16 window installations with stark white materials. Whilst in an austere palette, the surrealist tapestry of rich texture illuminates characteristic of each featured product.

DE & SE: Bonsoir Paris

AD & CL: Galeries Lafayette

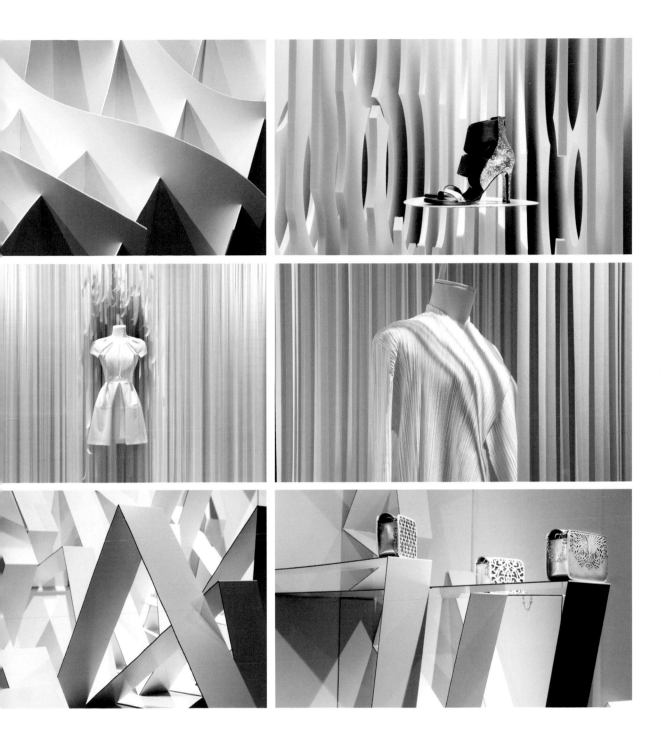

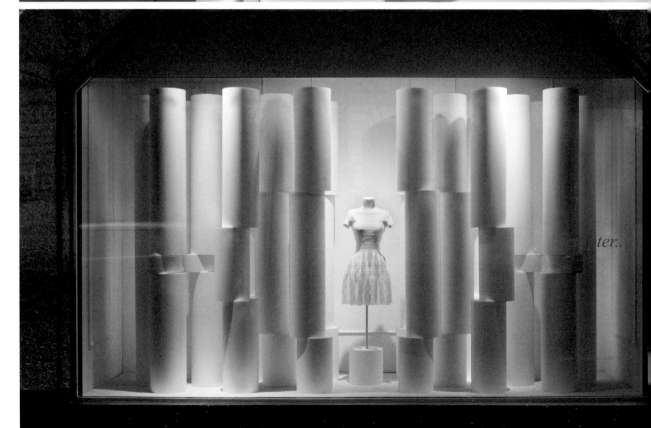

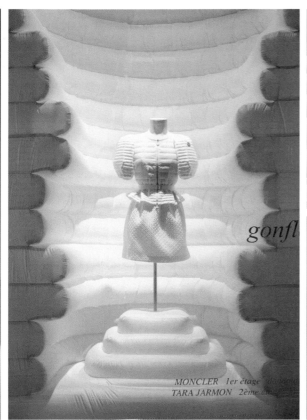

gonfl

MONCLER 1er étage *dancing*
TARA JARMON 2ème étage

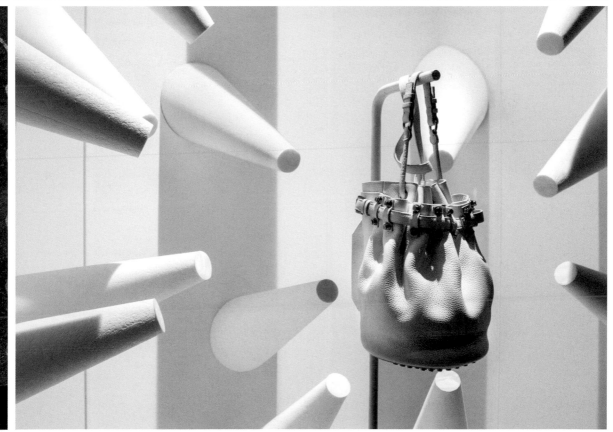

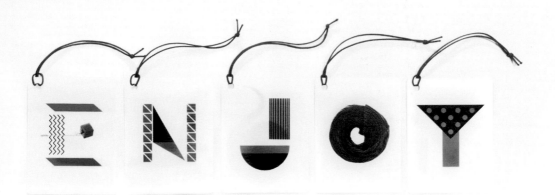

ISSEY MIYAKE MESSAGE

Issey Miyake's festive MESSAGE for 2014 was not at all a flat statement. Incorporating the elements of transformation, dimension, and the flat, MESSAGE conveyed the brand's philosophy in a spatial installation. Perceivable as a typeface from the shop's front, and a colour-themed scatter of items from other points. Individual alphabets was also printed as gift tags that allow shoppers to assemble words or messages.

DE: TYMOTE

CL: ISSEY MIYAKE INC.

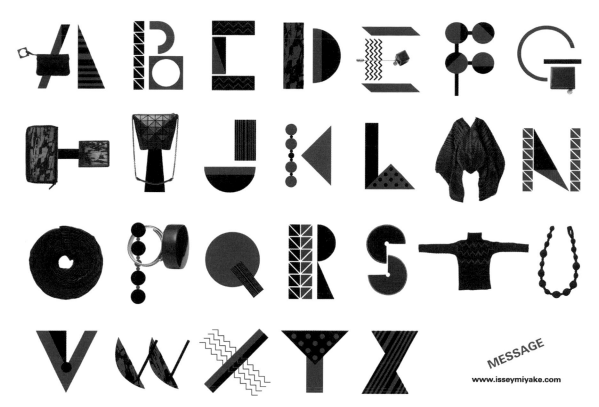

MESSAGE

www.isseymiyake.com

ELTTOB TEP

ISSEY MIYAKE

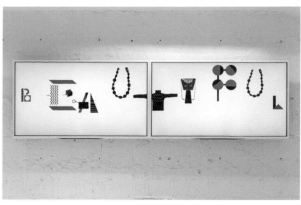

CH-AIR-S FOR ISSEY MIYAKE

Carrying through Issey Miyake's philosophy, which is creating fashion by adding dimensions in clothes, yoichi yamamoto architects devised a window display setting founded on optical illusion. What looked like random floating sticks and lines illustrated a much different view as viewers walked across the shop window. Chairs were assembled when looked at up front. On top of being a playful interpretation, the suspending panels were also display shelves for the brand's latest collection.

DE: yoichi yamamoto architects

CL: ISSEY MIYAKE INC.

CO: moph INC.

2D/3D CHAIRS FOR ISSEY MIYAKE

yoichi yamamoto architects' window display for Issey Miyake's Spring/
Summer 2011 collection was a combination of 2D floor paintings and physical
sculptures. The deceptively melting blue chairs rendered the transformation
of forms, as Issey Miyake portrayed in his clothing designs. Drawings on the
floor of the window display stretched to complete the chairs in dimension
when viewed at the right angle. On the other hand, the chair's backs
functioned as a hook to showcase the season's hats.

DE: yoichi yamamoto architects

CL: ISSEY MIYAKE INC.

CO: moph INC.

SPACE DIPPED SHIRTS

A paradigm of simplicity and subtlety, a classic crisp white shirt took central stage at Milan Salone 2014 as a COS-nendo crossover piece. Bit by bit dropped in and pulled out of hollowed steel cube sculptures, neatly lined up shirts floated through rooms and took on gradated colours as if the space inside the frames dyed the shirts. Where frames and shirts interplayed, the illusion effect raised the awareness of the space for the audience.

DE: nendo

CL: COS

PH: Daici Ano, Takumi Ota

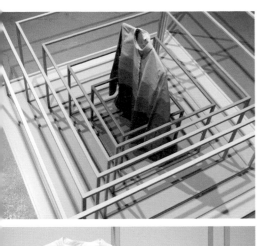

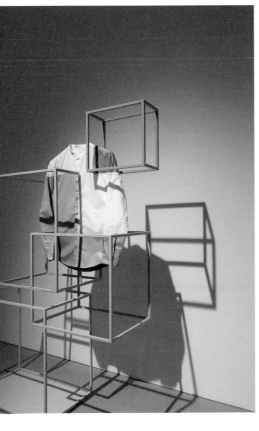

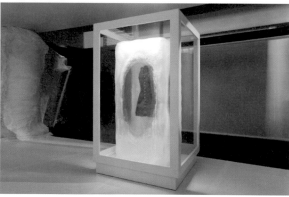

The Statement Dri-FIT black mesh dress offers Seren...
moisture wicking properties in a beautiful style
with two layers of Dri-FIT stretch mesh to keep her dry
and cool on the court. The dress is accented with satin
trim and stud detailing around the waist, arms and
neck with a dramatic line of snaps down the front.

NIKE SERENA WILLIAMS US OPEN NYC

US Open guests and members of the media were able to sense what Nike
had created for Serena Williams without clothing themselves in it. Highly
breathable and moisture repelling, the new fabric used in the world tennis
champion's tennis dress was designed to keep her comfortably cool during
the game, despite the dark colour and the scorching hot weather outside.
The immersive environment boosted a sense of lightness by transforming the
venue into an ice museum.

DE: ceft and company new york

CL: Nike inc.

SE: Tom Bell

NIKE SNEAKERBALL SCULPTURE

Specially commissioned for Nike World Basketball Festival 2014, the massive concrete Sneakerball added tactility to the event's theme "Come Out In Force" conceived by agency Rosie Lee. Sneakers in the sculpture depicted Air Jordan 1, Nike Air Force 1 and Nike Blazer, the first three basketball sneakers ever created by Nike. The design worked both in print and as a striking selfie spot next to the brand's overarching campaign. The event took place at Palaciao Cibeles in Madrid, Spain.

DE: Shane Griffin

CL: Nike Netherlands

CR: Rosie Lee London, Ruben PB (PH)

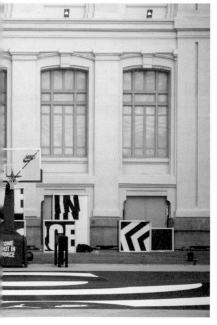

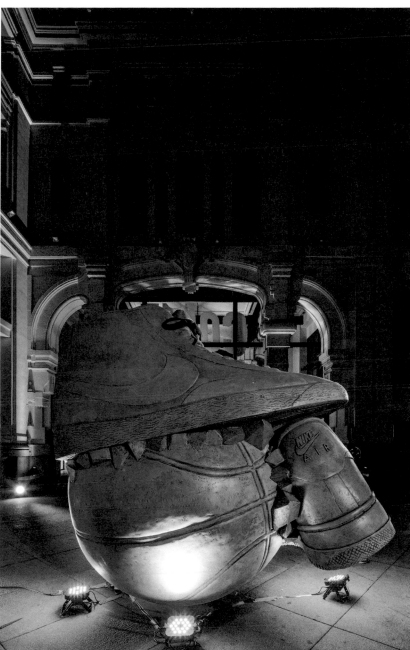

B I O GRAPHY

...,STAAT CREATIVE AGNECY

An international creative agency based in Amsterdam, the Netherlands, ...,staat works with both local leaders and global brands delivering fully integrated branding concepts. Established in 2000, the original thinkers of the agency turn everyday into the iconic, from strategy to concept to design, with no limits and passion.

&LARRY

Whether commercial or experimental, &Larry approaches each project with a desire to create works that are honest, functional and expressive beyond aesthetics. The studio has adopted the Eames motto of "Take your pleasure seriously" and this philosophy can be seen in a diverse body of work that includes film posters as well as a series of intriguing Singapore-inspired Objects.

ACMÉ PARIS

Created by Elodie Mandray and Caroline Aufort, Paris-based Acmé Paris is a graphic design studio specialising in art direction, print, visual identity and typography. The studio works in close ties with clients from defining each project's scope to production. The hand-crafted dimension is a quality pledge for them. The infinity of possible combinations and inherent restraint of each project have turn into their playground, where they evolve in constant search of meaning. The studio's objective is to reach out to the Acmé.

ALMEIDA, CARLA

Multidisciplinary designer, art director and lecturer from Porto, Portugal. Almeida freelances for a variety of clients in Portugal and abroad. Graduated in Communication Design at Portuguese Art and Design School (FSAD), Almeida became a member of Visual Communication Department of FABRICA — Benetton's Communication Research Centre in Treviso, Italy in 2006. She was also a speaker at 2013 World Graphics Day.

BONSOIR PARIS

A multi-media creative agency founded in early 2010 by Remy Clémente and Morgan Maccari, after studying at Duperré and at the Gobelins, Bonsoir Paris' state of mind is to shake usual borders, balancing between logic and absurdity, art and design. They like to play with gravity and marry materials that don't usually belong together, yet simple as every good idea should be. Whether it is design (volumetric or graphic), image (photography and film), digital experiences, or branding, the research-driven creative studio seeks to fade its disciplinary practices in order to challenge its creative limits.

BUREAU COLLECTIVE

Bureau Collective is a design studio founded in 2009 by Ollie Schaich and Ruedi Zürcher in St.Gallen. We like to work in the different fields of graphic design and enjoy working with people who are as passionate about what they do as we are. We share our studio with a photographer (Ladina Bischof), as well as another small graphic design studio (Kasper-Florio). So we enjoy the opportunity of personal exchange and the benefit of using the infrastructure together. We aim to have fun at work and develop stand-alone products, in which our personality flows into. For this reason we are especially interested in the experimental field and creative freedom.

CEFT AND COMPANY NEW YORK

Founded in 2003, ceft and company new york was conceived as a creative lab structured to solve communication and marketing challenges without the limits imposed by preconceived mediums that generally limit traditional agencies. The all-rounded agency was created not to duplicate yet another agency, but because what was desperately needed did not exist.

CIUCIULKAITE, EGLE

A young graduate in graphic design at Vilnius Academy of Arts, Ciuciulkaite is interested in everything related to design and art, including dancing and piano playing. Ciuciulkaite's work is mostly concentrated on branding and packaging design, while it's also close to illustration.

CLASE BCN

Clase Bcn is a graphic design and visual communication studio in Barcelona made up of a team of young, international, multidisciplinary professionals whose work has won a number of awards. They work on all areas of design but pay particular attention to typeface and the element of surprise.

CMOK, DAWID

Graduated in graphic design at the Academy of Fine Arts in Katowice, Poland, graphic design and street art has been Cmok's passion and inspiration. His work is featured in many books, magazines and websites around the world. In recent years, Cmok has taken part in many exhibitions and graffiti/street art festivals.

DI GENNARO, DAVIDE, BUFFA, PIETRO

Two Italian graphic designers based in Milan, Italy. Gennaro and Buffa work to focus on visual identity and editorial projects, both analogue and digital.

DORLOT, EVAN

Moving from Paris to Prague since 2012, Dorlot is a graduate in graphic design at la Fonderie de l'image, Paris while also holding an associate degree with print specialty. Prior to be a freelancer, Dorlot was an art director for a Parisian communication agency who works with notorious international firms such as Total, Air France, and BNP Parisbas.

DORMER VOLGSTEN, ANNA

Dormer Volgsten is currently a fine arts student focusing on visual communication at Beckmans College of Design in Stockholm, Sweden.

EMPATÍA®

Operating in a global marketplace, the Argentinian-based design agency work closely with clients to make brands alive and profitable. empatía® seeks the highest possible design quality down to the last detail. Simple yet long lasting, their design is environmental contributing towards economic and social sustainability.

EPS51 GRAPHIC DESIGN STUDIO

An internationally active design studio developing visual concepts with a strong focus on typography and bilingual design, Eps51 has worked on numerous intercultural projects mostly for clients from the fields of culture, design and fashion. Founders Ben Wittner and Sasca Thoma regularly take part in exhibitions, give lectures and hold workshops.

ESKIMO DESIGN STUDIO

One of the leading Russian design studios, Eskimo's creative services cover logo design, brand identity, web design, etc. The team works with clients all over the world, creating clear ideas with a strong visual language for diverse brands.

FIRMALT

Firmalt is a multidisciplinary creative agency based in Monterrey, Mexico that provides unique solutions for developing and positioning brands by creating strong visual concepts that communicate clear ideas, add values, and differentiate from the competitions.

GRIFFIN, SHANE

An Irish visual artist, designer, and director currently based in New York City, Griffin's portfolio exhibits a broad range of visual mediums, such as film, design, sculpture, and animation. A unique blend of technically crafted and aesthetically considered imagery, his style is always evolving, as it blurs the lines between commercial advertising and art.

HIGH TIDE

High Tide is an independent design studio that creates compelling visual narrative through innovative and interactive media tools. Their work ranges from branding and marketing projects to limited edition publications and site-specific installations. Founder Danny Miller received his B.F.A. from UCLA before returning to New York to work as an art director at Atlantic Records. In 2009, Miller founded the Bear Cave, working with global brands such as Nike and Heineken.

HYPE TYPE STUDIO

Formed in 1999 by Paul Hutchison, Hype Type is a multidisciplinary graphic design and communications studio with experience extends across the art, consumer goods and services, government, healthcare, media and entertainment, music, fashion and many more. The studio's clients include Nike, Quiksilver, MTV, British Energy, Jeff Lewis Design, Mark Tessier Landscape Architect, ESPN, Stussy, and more.

I.T APPARELS LTD.

I.T traces its beginnings back to a simple idea: to cater the young individuals with a distinct sense of style. The devoted following that grew from this has made its name synonymous with young fashion at the cutting edge. Individuals behind the I.T story are driven by a simple passion to bring names both recognised and experimental to successive generations of customers.

INT WORKS

As an integral part of It's Nice That, INT Works inherently understands what's happening on the cutting edge of creativity. From the most successful and innovative content, to the best ideas and talent working in the world today; insight and inspiration are at their fingertips. With years of experience in making cross-platform content from strategy to delivery, the award-winning creative content and communications agency harnesses this expertise to help brands communicate messages in effective and engaging ways.

IYA STUDIO

Working across multiple disciplines and platforms to engage customers in an exciting and innovative way, IYA Studio collaborates with clients and shares passion and knowledge with them. The independent creative studio develops products and stories through engaging design and communication.

JANSSON, JOAKIM

Founder of independent design studio Sans Colour, the Swedish graphic designer is currently based in New York, USA.

JESPERS, JELLE

Born in Antwerp, Belgium in 1976, Jespers is a graphic designer who studied 3D and Multimedia design at KASK Ghent. He started his own office in 2005 and has mainly been working for cultural institutions and the fashion industry.

KNIPF, TOBIAS

Knipf is a graphic designer, filmmaker, photographer and one half of animation- & design-duo Musclebeaver with Andreas Kronbeck. He lives and works in Munich, Germany.

STUDIO PAOLO BAZZANI

Bazzani's studio focuses on graphic arts projects and art direction for the fashion industry. A close friend of Antonio Marras since the early nineties, Bazzani has a long working relationship with the fashion designers' brand as well as KENZO that was creative directed by Marras back then. Bazzani loves to explore the use of unique materials and unusual shapes that make the message particularly striking. He also designs sets for events and theatre.

STUDIO SP-GD

Founded in 2010 by Surya Prasetya, Studio SP-GD works with a diverse range of clients from the public and commercial sectors, developing innovative solutions for print, digital and environmental media. The Melbourne-based graphic design studio believes collaborative, innovative and content-led solutions give their clients the most appropriate solutions. Each projects character and goals is followed by an analytical process resulting in a bespoke solution fit to each clients' specific needs.

STUDIOSMALL

Providing creative and strategic art direction for branding, identity, digital, literature, packaging and environments, StudioSmall is experienced across fashion, luxury, lifestyle, design and hospitality sectors worldwide for international clients that include Alfred Dunhill, Comme des Garçons, Margaret Howell, BAFTA, Anglepoise and Johnnie Walker.

SUBLIMA COMUNICACIÓN

Sublima was founded in 2002 in the city of Murcia, Spain, as a creative communication agency, but it rather calls itself "a company of ideas".

TANNIA & AHMAD

Tannia Surijadjaja and Ahmad Fauzan are two Indonesian-born designers who graduated in communication design. Both graphic designers and illustrators, they enjoy experimenting and working together through the love of still-life styling and photography.

THE ESLITE SPECTRUM CORPORATION, CHUANG, MENG-TANG

The Eslite Spectrum holds "humanities, the arts, creativity, and lifestyle" as its core values. It focuses on the management of Eslite's lifestyle and culture outlets in Taiwan and Hong Kong. Meng-Tang Chuang is an art designer in the office of the Eslite Spectrum in Taipei. The designer studied Book Arts at Camberwell College of Arts, University of the Arts London.

THE STRANGELY GOOD

A spatial, branding and graphic design agency, The Strangely Good is a tad outrageous and categorically devoted to creating the not-so-everyday idea. The team thrives on brand new perspectives to deliver extraordinary ideas. that are not only beautifully thoughtful but also felicitously crafted.

THINGSIDID

A Hong Kong-based creative studio committed in branding, print, graphics, packaging for clients from corporate, retail, art and culture.

TWO TIMES ELLIOTT

A design consultancy based in Notting Hill, London, Two Times Elliott produces a diverse range of work across multiple disciplines including print design, identity and web. They interpret and convey clients' messages clearly and intelligently.

TYMOTE

Established in 2008, TYMOTE has been engaging in many different categories of client projects and producing art works such as graphic design, motion, music, and programming. Their overarching goal is to be the "Pirates of design".

VALLÉE DUHAMEL

Founded by Julien Vallée and Eve Duhamel, the studio creates images and videos for a wide range of clients from events to commercials, music, fashion, posters, magazines and objects. Vallée Duhamel specialises in high quality, lo-fi, and often handmade visuals and installations, and favours a playful and experimental approach toward work.

VANDENBERGH, LAURA LÉ

Vandenbergh is a London-based designer and art director, with a passion for design, fashion, art and pineapples. Studied at both the Royal Academy of Fine Arts in Antwerp, and the Central Saint Martins University of Arts in London, Vandenbergh is the creative director of Studio Lé, next to her job as a senior designer and art director at Liberty London. Combining her advertising, retail and fashion background, Vandenbergh creates unique concepts that understands clients needs from both an aesthetically and commercial point of view.

VEAZEY, JOSEPH

After his junior year at Savannah College of Art and Design, Veazey's internship at Adult Swim of Cartoon Network in Atlanta led to a full-time job doing graphic design and illustration after he finished school. In 2012, Veazey moved to New York City where he has been doing freelance work and assisting his girlfriend with the launch of her fashion label, Azede Jean-Pierre. He is currently an art director and designing prints for the label, which is now entering its fourth season.

VIOLAINE & JÉRÉMY

An illustration and graphic design studio based in Paris, France, Violaine Orsoni and Jérémy Schneider are a team of artistic directors, graphic designers and illustrator. From fabric pattern design to magazine design or brand identity, Violaine & Jérémy works with different industry sectors including fashion brands like Dior, FrenchTrotters, and le Coq Sportif; cultural institution such as the National Orchestra of Lorraine and Influencia Magazine; luxury names such as Tiffany and Co.; and music label like Ekler'o'shock.

VUOTI, AINO-MARIA LOVIISA

Born in a city of Oulu, Finland, and graduated from Lahti University of Applied Sciences Institute of Design and Fine Arts, Vuoti is working as a freelancer and has spent summers as a graphic designer trainee at Stora Enso Packaging Oy.

WALKER, SEAN

Walker is a freelance graphic designer based in Wellington, New Zealand specialising in print media.

WANG, JIAJIE ROGER

The graphic designer has worked for some world-renowned firms such as Interbrand and Lunar Design after studying in San Francisco. Being influenced by Asian culture, Wang's works ingeniously combined Western and Eastern elements, providing clarity and creativity. His solid understanding of branding has helped his clients better communicate with their audiences. Wang always seeks for something new and ready to dive in.

WANITZEK, CAROLIN & ADELMANN, DENNIS

Two communication designers and photographers based in Mannheim, Germany, Carolin Wanitzek and Dennis Adelmann got in touch during their communication design study and discovered their passion for design and photography.

WELKER, MORITZ

Welker is a Munich-based designer with a strong focus on typography and concept-driven works in web and print.

WHITTINGHAM, ROSALIE KATE

An illustrator currently based in London, UK who mainly focuses on portraiture and fashion illustration, the artist likes to mix digital work with detailed hand-drawn techniques to create a unique signature style which is easily transformed and reworked.

YAGO, NAONORI

Born in Shizuoka, Japan in 1986, Yago graduated in visual communication at Musashino Art University in 2009 and joined Hakuhodo as a designer in the same year. Yago disclosed the original art work "PAPER LEAF" in 2012 and put on a solo exhibition with large-scale installation at a 250 m² gallery in Tokyo. She has received numerous awards such as Silver prize in Young Lotus (2012), D&AD inbook (2014), Tokyo TDC nominate(2014), and New York ADC Bronze (2014).

YOICHI YAMAMOTO ARCHITECTS

After finishing the graduate course at Waseda University, Yoichi Yamamoto, who was born in 1975, joined the Design Division of Shimizu Corporation and met Yayoi Ito, who was born in 1979 and graduated from Japan Women's University. Yamamoto founded yoichi yamamoto architects in 2006 and Ito has worked there since then. The firm has won numerous awards such as JCD Design Award and Rookie Award in 2008, CS Design Award and Semi-Gran Prix in 2012.

ZIEGER, MARIE

Zieger is a lettering artist, editorial aficionado and graphic designer working and living in Graz, Austria. She has been freelancing and collaborating with different studios on brand identities, book projects and custom letterings. Zieger is in love with script fonts, role-playing video games, mockumentaries, crafting neat digital mixtapes and getting all amateurishly nerdy with mobile photography.

ACKNOWLEDGEMENTS

We would like to thank all the designers and companies who have
involved in the production of this book. This project would not have been
accomplished without their significant contribution to the compilation
of this book. We would also like to express our gratitude to all the
producers for their invaluable opinions and assistance throughout this
entire project. The successful completion also owes a great deal to
many professionals in the creative industry who have given us precious
insights and comments. And to the many others whose names are not
credited but have made specific input in this book, we thank you for your
continuous support the whole time.

FUTURE EDITIONS

If you wish to participate in viction:ary's future projects and publications,
please send your website or portfolio to submit@victionary.com